D1485623

OLYMPICS 1984

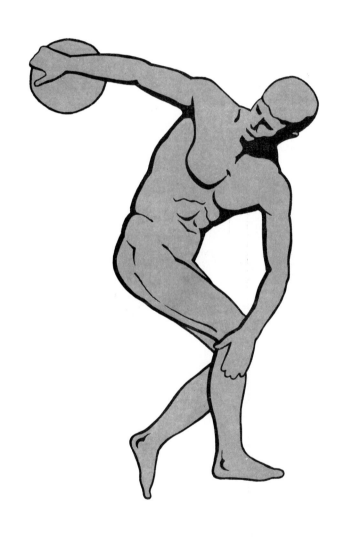

Produced for Philips International B.V.
by Marshall Cavendish Books Limited
58 Old Compton Street
London W1V 5PA

© Philips International B.V., Jarrold
and Sons Limited and Marshall Cavendish
Limited 1984

Author: Martin Tyler
Executive Editor: Keith Faulkner
Assistant Editor: James Harrison
Designer: Jonathan Lambert
Production: Dennis Hovell/Richard Churchill

Consultant Editor: Phil Soar
Authenticator: Maurice Golesworthy

Publishing Director: Nicolas Wright

Printed in England by
Jarrold and Sons Limited

OLYMPICS 1984

LE PRÉSIDENT

The flame is lit and the oath read : "In the name of all competitors I promise that we will take part in these Olympic Games, respecting and abiding by the rules which govern, in the true spirit of sportsmanship, for the glory of sport and the honour of our teams."

Thus begins the Olympic Games, the world's greatest sporting occasion. Nothing else compares with its international appeal and its intensity of competition; no other event brings together so many nationalities in such brotherhood and harmony. And for the individual, nothing else compares with the glory of winning a gold.

But not everyone can win a gold, or indeed a silver or bronze medal. For them the achievement is merely to have taken part and to have had the honour of representing their country on the world's stage.

This handsome volume, seeks to portray something of the excitement, the glamour, the striving and the sheer skill involved in the modern Olympic Games. From track events to water sports; from fencing to gymnastics, the contents reflect the Olympic ideal, which is, after all, the pursuit of sporting excellence.

Juan Antonio SAMARANCH
President
International Olympic Committee

CONTENTS

THE OLYMPIC STORY

Despite the difficulties of keeping its identity in a society that has undergone massive change during the 88-year history of the competition, the Olympic Games still stands supreme as the ultimate sporting occasion.

Despite those countries and individuals who have tried to usurp it as a political platform – and even threatened to jeopardize its very existence – the modern Olympic Games continue to represent a truly global sporting spectacle, first inspired by Baron de Coubertin in 1896.

Despite an unfashionable quality in today's values of the Olympic ideal, "taking part is more important than winning", the sporting circus which pitches its tents in Los Angeles in July 1984 has still kept its distance from total professionalism.

At its best the Games remains a joyous celebration of athletic activity, embracing the best young talents from every point on the circumference of the globe. For all the withdrawals from recent competitions, no sporting gathering is more truly international. The challenge to maintain the dignity and the stature of the Olympics now rests with the organisers in Los Angeles, whose

Below: The start of it all, the starting-line at Athens! The initiative of Baron Pierre de Coubertin led to the first modern Games in 1896.

Left: The opening ceremony at Stockholm in 1912. In Sweden the Games were excellently organised, with particular credit to Sigfrid Edstrom who later became President of the International Olympic Committee.

Below: Despite the difficulties in preparing for the Games after the ravages of World War I, the Antwerp Olympics of 1920 were a great success. Germany, and their allies in the recent conflict, were not invited.

task, above all else, is to keep the competition viable against
economic – as well as political – pressures.

In the history of the tournament – both distant and recent – many
such obstacles have been faced and overcome, with the same will
to win that has characterised generations of Olympic performers.
De Coubertin had to seek victory in the first battle of all, to revive
interest in the idea of such a spectacle which had found great
favour in the culture of the Ancient Greeks. Athens, then, was a
suitable venue for the opening of the modern Games in 1896.
Records vary, but it is commonly agreed that 311 athletes took part
representing 13 nations. From that small acorn a huge tree grew.
In 1900 at Paris and 1904 at St. Louis some impetus was lost. Both
Games were staged as part of a wider festival, the World's Fair.
The events were strung out over several months. Some
competitors did not even realise that they were taking part in the
Olympics. De Coubertin was so disappointed that he instituted
another Games in 1906 in Athens, with thoughts of a permanent
site there. History now notes these as Interim Games, because
two years later another Olympiad took place, in London rather
than Rome because the Italian government withdrew their offer

*Below left: One Mexican's view of
the Olympics coming to town. The
stone slab decorated to
commemorate the Games at
Mexico City in 1968.*

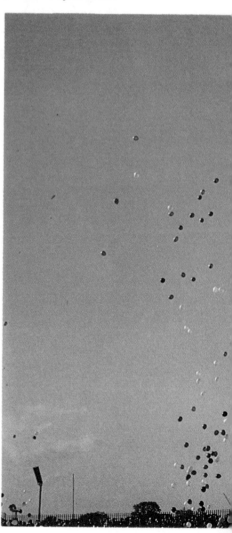

Left: The 1968 Games were staged in Mexico City in October when their summer rainy season was supposed to have passed!

Below: Tokyo had to wait 24 years for its Olympic celebration. The city had been chosen for the cancelled 1940 Games.

in the aftermath of the eruption of the volcano Vesuvius.
Just when the routine of the four-year cycle had been established
– in Stockholm in 1912 more than one million spectators
witnessed a very well-run tournament – World War I crushed any
hopes of a 1916 Olympics.

With Belgium still recovering from the devastation of the
invasion, Antwerp's selection in 1920 came as a surprise. Antwerp
gave the Games the Olympic flag, the interlinked five rings. For
the first time, too, the ceremony included the oath pledged by the
athletes:
"In the name of all the competitors I promise that we shall take
part in these Olympic Games, respecting and abiding by the rules
which govern them, in the true spirit of sportsmanship, for the
glory of sport and honour of our teams."
Amsterdam, the selected venue in 1924, yielded to de Coubertin's
wishes for Paris to be given a second chance to stage the Games
after the debacle of 1900. Holland, however, was the choice in
1928 where the tournament was marked by the inclusion, after
considerable debate, of track and field events for women.

Right: Though the teams parade as countries, and team events play an important part in the Olympic Games, the essence of this sporting occasion is individual competition. In fact, medal tables illustrating the successes of each nation are unofficial.

Below: The pageantry of the opening ceremony where national costumes as well as the athletes are on display.

Below right: Competitors of all hues and colours, epitomise the international nature of the Olympic Games.

As the organisers of the 1984 Los Angeles Games contemplate the problems they face, they can find inspiration in what that city achieved in 1932. The world was suffering from the Depression at that time and the distance to California seemed prohibitive. The invention of the Olympic Village, where the competitors could be housed collectively and cheaply, solved the dilemma. Ironically there will be no Olympic Village for the 1984 Games.

Heavy clouds of propaganda hung over the 1936 experience. Berlin's Olympics became a vehicle for Adolf Hitler and the Third Reich. Germany responded to the Führer's call by finishing as the most successful nation at the Games with a total of 89 medals. One item of Olympic tradition was established; for the first time runners transported the torch from Olympia to light the flame.

After World War II London took aboard the Games for a second time, while an impressive organisation in Helsinki in 1952 helped the Olympic movement back into full swing. Four years later Melbourne provided the first venue in the Southern Hemisphere, and the latest start in the year, November 22nd.

Below: The Olympic flame presiding over the 1972 yachting centre at Kiel in West Germany

Left: After the march-past comes the gathering of nations, in the traditional manner, in the centre of the Olympic Stadium. In 1928 at Amsterdam the surrounds of the stadium were so packed that some athletes had to scale the walls to get inside to take part in the opening ceremony.

Italy finally got its Olympics in 1960, fifty-two years after it was first selected; Rome not only welcomed tremendous spectators but also television coverage which is now an accepted part of the institution of the Games. Tokyo took its turn in 1964 — the Japanese capital had been the choice for the cancelled 1940 tournament. In Asia the Games flourished.

Mexico City was a far less appreciated venue in 1968. Its rarified atmosphere sparked exceptional performances from those used to altitude; others suffered in desperate need of oxygen and the impression left was of unfair competition.

In 1972 Munich provided one peak – a record 122 nations and 7156 participants – and one fearful tragedy, the death of eleven hostages.

The very survival of the Games was threatened but, as it had shown in the past, it weathered this political storm only to face serious financial problems at Montreal where the stadia were not ready and the loss came to £700 million; it also weathered the African boycott in 1976 and the anti-Afghanistan invasion boycott against the Russians in 1980, when the United States, West Germany, and Japan were prominent among the withdrawals.

Below and right: Montreal's Olympic facilities with their innovative styles were not fully ready for the 1976 Games; the delay had been caused by building strikes.

Individuals have used the Games for their own political statements, notably Tommie Smith and John Carlos, the two Americans who gave the Black Power salute at the 200 metres victory ceremony in Mexico City in 1968. Vince Matthews and Wayne Collett, also from the United States, made similar gestures on the rostrum in 1972.

The International Olympic Committee is constantly scrutinising the difference between sponsored and professional athletes, as commercialisation plays an increasing part in the make-up of the Games. The illegal use of drugs and stimulants is another area which the IOC is determined to eradicate.

Great efforts have been made to make Los Angeles 1984 a self-sufficient Olympics which will provide a safer formula for

Right: Moscow's opening ceremony surpassed the considerable inventiveness of previous occasions. A close study of this formation in the centre of the Lenin Stadium illustrates the co-ordination between hundreds of young gymnasts. All rehearsals took place behind locked doors, and the revelation made the world gasp on July 19th 1980.

Left: Three Moscow scenes with the central picture created and changed by coloured cards held by superbly trained Russians. Overleaf: Opening day in 1972. One hundred and twenty-two competing nations assembled in Munich's distinctive stadium.

those who take on the massive responsibility in the future. Only two new stadia have been constructed; the swimming-pool built by McDonalds, the hamburger chain, and the velodrome financed by Southland, who own the 7-Eleven stores. As in 1932 the Coliseum will be the centre-piece for the ceremonies and the track and field events. The considerable facilities of the city's major universities have been utilised to avoid any unnecessary expenditure; the business footing is vital with no government subsidies to rely on, while lotteries, used to help finance past Olympics, are illegal under the state law of California.

More than 40 companies have been licensed to use the Olympic symbol in sponsorship deals that should raise at least £130 million. Such attention to detail should avoid the one often-recalled hiccough at Los Angeles in 1932 when the steeplechasers were asked to run one lap too many and Joe McCluskey (United States) was passed on the extra circuit to finish third instead of second.

The 14th Winter Olympics in Sarajevo were a reminder that the summer Games are not their sum total of this galaxy of sporting stars. They are, though, the focal point, the justification of the Olympic ideal. If the glamorous trappings are cast aside, the raw competition – individual against individual, may the best man win – remains the essential appeal of the greatest show on earth . . .

Below: Olympic competition returns to the Los Angeles Memorial Coliseum, 52 years after it housed the 1932 Olympics.

Below: The rowing events at Los Angeles in 1984 will take place here at Lake Casitas, 84 miles north-west of the Coliseum.

Left: In the absence of public or government funds, big business has been wooed to finance the 1984 Games by exclusive sponsorship deals. The new Olympic Pool has been built by McDonalds of hamburger fame.

MEN'S ATHLETICS

The athletics track is the centrepiece of every Olympic Games. The spotlight shines somehow brighter on a victorious runner. The struggle to be first across the line epitomises the sporting battle.

Each Olympiad produces track stars who inspire a generation — Nurmi . . . Owens . . . Zatopek . . . Snell . . . Viren . . . Juantorena. In a vast list of Olympic triumph, names like theirs' will always stand out. Who will join the elite in Los Angeles? The appeal of that question is fundamental to the appeal of the Olympic Games. The short sprint titles are regarded as proof of "the fastest man on earth", even though many of these Olympic records have stood since 1968; at Mexico City James Hines won the final of the 100 metres in 9.95 seconds. The thin air of Mexico City also produced records at 200 metres by Tommie Smith (United States), 400 metres by Lee Evans (United States) and 1500 metres by Kip Keino (Kenya) which still stand.

Seven sprinters have accomplished the double of 100 and 200 metres in the same Games: Archie Hahn (United States) 1904, Ralph Craig (United States) 1912, Percy Williams (Canada) 1928, Eddie Tolan (United States) 1932, Jesse Owens (United States) 1936, Bobby-Joe Morrow (United States) 1956, and Valery Borzov (Soviet Union) 1972.

Right: Contender for the fastest sprint — Carl Lewis. Will black American sprinters continue their sprinting successes at the Los Angeles Games?

Right: The photo-finish technique has electronically ended arguments like that over the 5000 metres at Los Angeles in 1932 when Lehtinen (Finland) was given a disputed win over Hill (United States).

Left: The thoroughbreds of the Olympic 400 metres. So intense is the level of competition that fractions of seconds determine whether years of dedication end as success or failure.

The longer sprint events also produce their great athletes. The 1924 400 metres final made Scotsman Eric Liddell one of the Games' folk-heroes. Liddell's decision not to compete in the 100 metres final – he was favourite for the event – because the heats were to be staged on a Sunday was a central story in the award-winning film *Chariots of Fire*. A rugby international who later became a missionary, Liddell entered the 400 metres instead and stormed to victory.

Alberto Juantorena became the first athlete to perform the Olympic double of 400 and 800 metres gold medals in 1976. He also represented Cuba in their Olympic basketball team. Juantorena achieved his success against fierce competition; Wyndham Halswelle had a much less demanding but a more controversial victory in the 1908 400 metres. Halswelle ran a re-run alone after one American finalist had been disqualified and two others pulled out in protest. Paavo Nurmi – with nine golds and three silvers from 1920 to 1928 – set a tradition of Finnish distance running which was continued by the remarkable Lasse Viren, winner of both 5000 and 10,000 metres in 1972 and 1976. Peter Snell – now a medical teacher at the University of Texas – brought double gold to New Zealand in 800 and 1500 metres in 1964. Emil Zatopek produced a magnificent treble at Helsinki, 5000 metres, 10,000 metres and marathon.

Right: Sebastian Coe outpaced the field for his gold medal in the Moscow 1500 metres. Trailing in his wake were Jurgen Straub (East Germany), who was second, and Steve Ovett (Coe's major British rival) who collected the bronze medal.

Left: Miruts Yifter (left), the ageless Ethiopian, succeeded Lasse Viren in 1980 with invincible running in the 5000 and 10,000 metres. At the time of the Moscow Games, Yifter was at least 33 and maybe as old as 36.

Left: David Hemery produced a powerful performance at altitude to win the 400 metres hurdles in 1968. Four years later he had to settle for the bronze medal behind John Akii-Bua (Uganda) a remarkable runner who supposedly came from a family of 43 children!

Overleaf: The special demands of the 3000 metres steeplechase where the barriers break up the natural rhythm of running. Amos Biwott and Kip Keino brought a Kenyan influence to this event in 1968 and 1972 respectively.

"The Olympics are unique. There is no job, no amount of power, no money to approach the meaning of the Olympic experience." The quote comes from Al Oerter, a unique performer himself. At Melbourne, Rome, Tokyo and Mexico City, he reigned supreme in the discus circle, defying a variety of conditions and in 1964 a serious rib injury.

Oerter's reign spanned 12 years but in one breathtaking moment another American, Bob Beamon, created a world record that has lasted even longer. At Mexico City Beamon almost jumped through the entire long jump pit; his astonishing leap of 29 feet $2\frac{1}{2}$ inches improved the previous best by a massive $21\frac{3}{4}$ inches.

Six of the present field events were on the first list of activities at Athens in 1896; the hammer was added in 1900, the javelin in 1906. The very first Olympic event was the triple jump (then called hop, step and jump); James Connolly (United States) was the recipient of the first winner's medal and Myer Prinstein (United States) was prominent among the early competitors; Prinstein won the long jump in 1904 and 1906 and the triple jump in 1900 and 1904; his two successes in 1904 were on the same day. Erik Lemming (Sweden) out-threw all challenges becoming Olympic javelin champion in 1906, 1908 and 1912.

Right: A medal candidate for Los Angeles? Willie Banks (United States) is a talented triple jumper who has also created a marvellous rapport with crowds all over the world.

Below: Bob Beamon training at Mexico City in 1968. With the benefit of altitude he created a world record of enormous proportions — 29 feet 2½ inches in the long jump.

The early Games of this century included two-handed throwing of the javelin, discus and shot, but these events had a short life. Another style of competition which has since passed into history was the standing-jump, in long jump, high jump and triple jump. Between 1900 and 1908 Ray Ewry (United States), who had developed his leg muscles to overcome a childhood paralysis, collected ten gold medals in the standing-jumps.

Scientific development in the materials used to make the pole has increased the heights of the pole vaults. In 1896 the winning height, from a competition with only five entrants, was 3.30 metres. The present Olympic record is 5.78 metres, held by Poland's Wladislaw Kozakiewicz. In 1936 the battle for the pole vault gold lasted 12 hours! In 1964, another 12 hours of competition passed before Fred Hansen (United States) finally produced the winning vault.

Apart from a victory in 1906 by a Frenchman, Fernand Gonder, the pole vault remained in American hands from 1896 until 1968. Since then, however, Nordwig (East Germany) and Slusarski and Kozakiewicz from Poland have been Olympic champions.

Right: Igor Ter-Ovansyan (Soviet Union), who was third in the long jump in 1960 and 1964. The Soviet Union had never won this event, but through the remarkable Viktor Saneyev the Russians had three successive triple-jump victories in 1968, 1972 and 1976. At 34 Saneyev also finished second in Moscow in 1980.

Left: The throw of an Olympic champion; Dainis Kula, (Soviet Union) the gold medallist in the javelin at the 1980 Games in Moscow.

Below: The distinctive roof of the Munich stadium and the night sky are the backdrop to the pole vault competition in 1972.

The Olympic high jump title provides a fascinating tale of the development of the field athlete over the span of the modern Games. Ellery Clark (United States) was the first champion in 1896 with a winning jump of 1.81 metres. Gerd Wessig leapt 2.36 metres in 1980 to win East Germany's first gold in the event. Styles too have varied considerably. Dick Fosbury (United States) was arguably the most inventive; ignoring the conventional western roll or straddle methods he created a technique by which he went over the bar headfirst and backwards. The technique – known as the 'flop' – made him Olympic champion at Mexico City. Walter Davis, another American was an even more courageous winner; he had overcome the childhood affliction of polio to triumph in the high jump of 1952.

Below: The first Olympic high jump champion, Ellery Clark, cleared less than 6 feet in the 1896 Games. In the 1980 Games, Gerd Wessig cleared over 7 feet 7 inches for an Olympic and World record.

Right: Sawdust and sand have now been replaced by softer and safer synthetic landing areas.

Below: Dick Fosbury revolutionised the high jump when he 'flopped' his way to victory at Mexico City.

Overleaf: A controlled landing in the long jump, the muscles of the upper body as important as the legs.

John Flanagan (United States) emigrated from Ireland and established the hammer as an Olympic event with three consecutive gold medals in 1900, 1904 and 1908 (it was not held at Athens in 1906). America, though, has not had a hammer champion since Hal Connolly at Melbourne.

Hungary have produced three victories with Joszef Czermak in 1952 and Gyula Zsivotsky in 1968, after their initial hammer success by Imre Nemeth in 1948. Twenty-eight years later Nemeth's son Miklos kept the family traditions alive with a gold in the javelin at Montreal.

Norway has never been among the great nations in field events, but in 1956 their first athletics gold medal came via the javelin. Egil Danielsen was certainly not among the favourites but he was not the first nor the last to be inspired by the stimulus of Olympic competition. Danielsen even set a world record with his winning throw of 85.71 metres.

Supremacy in the shot is contested between the United States and Eastern European nations. Parry O'Brien, champion in 1952 and 1956 and runner-up in 1960, was at the core of American domination after World War II. Poland, East Germany and Russia have taken the last three gold medals.

Right: The mighty Al Oerter, whose four consecutive discus victories are an unparalleled achievement. He improved in each competition from 1956 to 1968 — from 56.36 metres in Melbourne to 64.78 metres, his winning throw at Mexico City.

Right: Hal Connolly, the 1956 hammer champion married Olga Fikotova, the women's discus champion from Czechoslovakia. Connolly chose the great Olympian Emil Zatopek to be his best man.

Right: Rothenburg of East Germany, exhibiting his power in the shot put. East Germany's first success in the event came from Udo Beyer, champion at Montreal in 1976.

Men's Athletics

From the great Jim Thorpe of the USA to GB's Daley Thompson, the decathlete has long been considered the superman of the Games. Ten events – 100 metres, long jump, shot put, high jump, 400 metres, 110 metres hurdles, discus, pole vault, javelin and 1500 metres – it is the track and field endurance test spread over two days.

Thorpe won the Stockholm Games of 1912, only to be disqualified because he had previously received a few dollars for playing professional baseball. In 1982, however, the IOC reinstated his victory, and the medal was finally presented to his family. Thompson, the 1983 World Champion and gold medallist in Moscow, has kept the decathlon in the limelight, fighting a succession of tremendous duels against West Germany's Jurgen Hingsen, with the world record regularly changing hands. The Olympic record, though, rests with the American Bruce Jenner, 8617 points in Montreal. Subsequently, Jenner was in great demand for endorsements and pursued a career as a television reporter, reflecting the universal appeal of the multi-event. Including Thorpe, Jenner's was the tenth success for the United States.

Below: Fierce rivalry in the decathlon. Daley Thompson of Great Britain (left) and Jurgen Hingsen from West Germany in dramatic conflict over 110m hurdles, a contest of pace and power.

Right: Bruce Jenner, the Olympic record holder, gold medallist in 1976 in Montreal.
Far right: The Moscow superathlete, Daley Thompson, hurls the javelin.

The marathon, 26 miles 385 yards, is steeped in the deep tradition of the Games. Based on the legendary run of Pheidippides, a Greek soldier, in 490BC, bearing the news to Athens that a Persian invasion had been repelled on the plains of Marathon, the endurance run was a natural for inclusion in the first modern Games in Athens in 1896. Appropriately enough it was won by another Greek messenger, Spiridon Louis, often incorrectly referred to as a shepherd. Louis was showered with gifts including free haircuts and groceries for life, for his triumph, and became very wealthy. As a married man, however, he could not collect the offer of one sponsor, who promised the hand of his daughter! The roll of honour includes marvellous victories by such great men as Emil Zatopek of Czechoslovakia at Helsinki in 1952; Abebe Bikila, the gallant Ethiopian who triumphed in Rome and Tokyo; Waldemar Cierpinski who brought dual success to East Germany in 1976 and 1980. It does not, however, tell the heartbreak of countless examples of brave running that were not enough; like Dorando Pietri, a tiny Italian, who led during the London Games in 1908, collapsed on the last lap, was helped across the line in first place, but then disqualified.
In Los Angeles, women, for the first time, take up the challenge.

Below: Rain can provide welcome respite in the pain of the marathon, where even finishing is a triumph.

Right: 1984 sees the first women's Olympic marathon. Grete Waitz has done so much to raise the standards of women's distance running.

Left: Waldemar Cierpinski, a physical education teacher from East Germany, accomplished a memorable double with Olympic marathon victories in 1976 and 1980. Cierpinski matched the achievement of Abebe Bikila who won in Rome and in Tokyo.

Left: Marathon running has become a craze in recent years, allowing even the fun-runners to line up with Olympians — at least at the start. In New York's annual event Alberto Salazar tastes victory.

Overleaf: Setting the early pace in the 1980 marathon are Michael Koussis (Greece) number 350, Vincent Rakabaele (Lesoto) number 479 and Emmanuel Mpioh (People's Republic of Congo) number 111.

Few events in Olympic history have started with such controversy as walking. In 1906 the 1500 metres ended in uproar with all the leaders disqualified for extending their walk into a run. George Bonhag (United States) strolled in, way down the field, to be declared the winner. A 3000 metres event was hastily arranged in a bid to quell the protests, only for more disqualifications to mar the proceedings. There were 3500 metres and 10 mile events in 1908.

The 3000 metres was put on again in 1920 – and won for Italy by Ugo Frigerio – and in five Games between 1912 and 1952 there were medals at stake over 10,000 metres. Since 1956 the 20,000 metres road walk has been staged, and, apart from 1976, there has been a 50,000 metres road walk since 1932.

In 1956 the gold medal in the 50,000 metres went to Norman Read representing New Zealand. Read certainly had a point to prove, after being rejected by his native British Olympic Association, and only included in the New Zealand squad at the last minute.

Another unlikely champion arrived in 1976. Mexico had no tradition and no gold medal in track and field until Daniel Bautista strode into the Olympic Stadium at Montreal at the head of 20,000 metres walk. Bautista's Olympic record was beaten by Maurizio Damilano (Italy), the winner in 1980 in 1hr 23:35.5.

Below: The Montreal Olympic Stadium was still under construction at the outset of the 1976 20 kilometres walk. The 50 kilometres event was dropped in 1976 but reinstated for the Moscow Games.

Above: Bernd Kannenberg
(no. 372) won the 50 kilometres
road walk in 1972, bringing
another gold medal for West
Germany at Munich.

Left: The cooling application of
the sponge, is as vital in
long-distance walking as in
marathon running.

WOMEN'S ATHLETICS _____

In the 1984 Olympic Games, women will compete over 400 metres hurdles, and 3000 metres, as well as in the marathon — another indication of the growth of track and field as a female sport. It is a development from a slow beginning, because it was not until 1928 that the best women runners in the world were accepted as part of the Olympics. The events then were restricted to 100 metres, 800 metres, 4 × 100 metres relay and high jump.

The participation was increased in 1932 and Mildred 'Babe' Didrikson (United States), who later became a renowned golfer, greatly increased the interest in women's sport with flamboyant successes in the 80 metres hurdles and javelin; she might have shared a gold in the high jump as well, but her style was controversially criticised by an official and she was awarded only second place.

The 200 metres was introduced at the London Games of 1948, where the women's competition found a dominant champion – Fanny Blankers-Koen of the Netherlands. One of the "immortals" of the Olympics, she took 4 gold medals – the 100 metres, 200 metres, 80 metres hurdles and 100 metres relay – at the age of 30.

Below: Annegret Richter (West Germany), the outstanding sprinter at Montreal, winning the 100 metres. She came second in the 200 metres.

Above right: Jarmila Kratochvilova, the 1983 world champion at 400 and 800 metres and Czechoslovakia's great hope for gold at Los Angeles.

Right: Evelyn Ashford (United States) a sprinter in the American tradition of former Olympic champions Wilma Rudolph and Wyomia Tyus.

Other women sprinters who ran their way into the Olympic record books include Marjorie Jackson (Australia) 1952, Betty Cuthbert (Australia) 1956, Wilma Rudolph (United States) 1960 and Renate Stecher (East Germany) 1972. They have all in turn emulated Fanny Blankers-Koen's distinction of winning the 100 and 200 metres at the same Olympic Games.

Another Australian, Shirley de la Hunty collected seven medals in all between 1948 and 1956, two golds in the 80 metres hurdles and another in the 4 × 100 metres relay. For sheer versatility and durability Irena Szewinska (Poland) has been a splendid example to aspiring young athletes. Her first Olympic competition was in Tokyo and, at 34, she was still competing at the Moscow Games. Her catalogue of medals reads: gold – 4 × 100 metres relay 1964, 200 metres 1968, 400 metres 1976; silver – long jump 1964, 200 metres 1964; bronze – 100 metres 1968, 200 metres 1972. That tally might have been even greater but she committed the cardinal sin of relay, dropping the baton, in the 4 × 100 metres at Mexico City.

Below: East Germany emerged as a potent force in women's track and field events in the 1970s. Among the successes were victories in the 4 × 100 metres in 1976 and 1980 and 4 × 400 metres in 1972 and 1976.

Right: More gold for East Germany at Moscow. Marita Koch, won the 400 metres, an event which was only introduced to the Games at Tokyo in 1964.

Left: Irena Szewinska (Poland) won her first gold medal under her maiden name Kirszentein in 1964, and was still competing in 1980.

Overleaf: The world's best women hurdlers face a new challenge at Los Angeles. For the first time there will be the 400 metres hurdles.

The first Olympic 1500 metre race for women took place at Munich. Ludmila Bragina (Soviet Union) gave the event a memorable baptism, breaking the world record in her heat, again in the semi-final and a third time in the final itself. Her winning time, 4:01.4, was 5.5 seconds better than her own pre-Games world best.

Another Russian, Tatyana Kazankina became a worthy successor to Bragina; Kazankina produced powerful victories in both 800 and 1500 metres at Montreal, and retained the latter title in 1980. The 1983 World Championships at Helsinki was another reminder of the immense improvement in women's distance running. Jarmila Kratochvilova (Czechoslovakia), Mary Decker (United States) and Grete Waitz (Norway) all performed with the potential of Olympic champions.

The short hurdles event was held over 80 metres until 1968: Irina Press (whose sister was a field event gold medal winner) triumphed in 1960. Since the lengthening to 100 metres, all the medals have gone to East European countries. East Germany's strength in depth has been emphasised by 4 × 100 metres relay wins in 1976 and 1980 and in the 4 × 400 metres in 1972 and 1976.

Below: A small woman with enormous talent. Tatyana Kazankina, (Soviet Union), 800 metres champion in 1976, 1500 metres champion at Montreal and Moscow.

Left: In the Helsinki World Championships in 1983, Mary Decker (United States) allied great charm to her successes in the 1500 and 3000 metres to become a favourite for Los Angeles.

Left: Renate Stecher's strong physique made her unbeatable in the 100 and 200 metres at Munich. In 1976 she took a silver and a bronze in the two sprints.

Women's Athletics

The first chapter in the history of women's field events in the Olympic Games was written by Halina Konopacka in 1928. The Polish girl threw the discus 39.62 metres, enough to win the gold medal at Amsterdam. Ethel Calderwood (Canada) leapt 1.59 metres in the high jump to become champion in the only other field competition for women at that time.

Micheline Ostermeyer was in the habit of entertaining her French team-mates with her most proficient piano-playing in between events. In 1948 her talented hands were totally in tune with the Olympic field events; originally chosen only for the shot put, which she duly won, Ostermeyer also entered the discus and though rated a total outsider she took a second gold. For another diversion she also took part in the high jump and finished third. Also on the discus list of winners is Olga Fikotova (Czechoslovakia) the 1956 champion, whose subsequent marriage to American Hal Connolly the men's hammer winner created such publicity the following year.

Right: Maria Petkova (Bulgaria) finished second in the discus in 1980, but she was more than two metres behind the winner, Evelin Jahl (East Germany).

Below: Olga Fikotova who found gold and a husband at Melbourne, and later competed as Olga Connolly. Her winning throw in the 1956 discus was 53.69 metres.

Right: Tamara, the elder of the Press sisters, was Olympic champion in the shot in 1960 and 1964, and also took the discus title at Tokyo.

The mighty Russian Tamara Press bestrode the Olympic stage in the early 1960s giving a foretaste of the formidable physiques women would develop for field events in the years to come. Press displayed her strength with a win in the shot at Rome, though she could only finish second in the discus behind Nina Ponomaryeva (Soviet Union). In 1964, however, she triumphed in both events. The youngest winner of an Olympic field event is Ulrike Meyfarth (West Germany) who, as a 16-year old, found herself embroiled in a tense high jump competition which would have wrecked many athletes with greater experience. In the 1972 Games Meyfarth did have the great advantage of the passionate support of the Munich crowd. She did not fail them in a lengthy contest with the Austrian world record holder Ilona Gusenbauer and Bulgaria's Yordanka Blagoyeva.

Blagoyeva was desperately unlucky when the bar fell after she had apparently cleared safely and was walking away from the pit. Meyfarth, however, ended any doubts by clearing 1.92 metres for a magnificent, if wholly unexpected, victory.

Right: Heide Rosendahl (West Germany) was a victim of illness at Mexico City, but her consolation at Munich included gold in the long jump and 4 × 100 metres relay, plus silver in the pentathlon.

Below: Ulrike Meyfarth only 16, the Olympic high jump champion at Munich. Four years later her failure was almost as spectacular as her success, when she failed to reach the final at Montreal.

The range in women's long jump has increased considerably from the days of Olga Gyarmati (Hungary), the winner in the initial year of 1948 with 5.69 metres to Tatyana Kolpakova (Soviet Union) who triumphed in Moscow with 7.06 metres. Viorica Viscopoleanu (Rumania) found the Mexico City altitude to her liking, as Bob Beamon did in the men's event, with a winning leap of 6.82 metres— a very impressive statistic for 1968.

Dana Zatopkova, wife of Emil Zatopek, was a popular winner of the javelin title at Helsinki bringing the total of family gold medals in 1952 to four. So far that has been Czechoslovakia's only success in the event in which Russia and East Germany have since won two gold medals each. Ruth Fuchs won for the East Germans in 1972 and 1976, but the 1980 champion came from a surprising source. Maria Colon threw 68.40 metres to give Cuba their first gold medal in women's track and field.

In 1968 the IOC instituted medical examination for women's events with sex-tests. Loss of femininity rather than female characteristics is a more common complaint. Long gone though is blatant impersonation like that of the German male who sneaked into the 1936 women's high jump. He only finished fourth!

Below: Maria Colon who inspired special celebration in Cuba in 1980 by winning the javelin competition at Moscow.

Left: Ruth Fuchs (East Germany) stood supreme in the women's javelin 1972 and 1976. At Munich her winning throw was 63.88 metres and at Montreal she improved to 65.94 metres.

Overleaf: In 48 years the power of women's javelin has increased by more than 50 percent, from Mildred Didrikson's 43.68 metres in 1932 to Maria Colon's 68.40 metres in 1980.

Women's Athletics

In 1964 Irina Press, the younger of the highly talented Russian sisters, marked the first Olympic woman's pentathlon with a total of 5246 points, then a world record.

The event, though, has altered. From 1964 to 1976 the five disciplines were hurdles (100 metres since 1972 but only 80 metres previously), shot put, high jump, long jump and 200 metres. In the Moscow Games the 800 metres was included in place of the sprint. In 1971 a new method of allocating points for performance replaced that which had brought gold medals for Press and Ingrid Becker of West Germany, the Mexico winner.

The development of women's athletics in the past decade has been reflected in an increase of the disciplines for the 1984 Games. As in the first track and field World Championships, the Pentathlon has grown into the Heptathlon, five events into seven. The extra two disciplines are the inclusion of the javelin and the return of the 200 metres. As in the pentathlon, the heptathlon will be staged over two days.

Below: Munich's triumphant trio! Mary Peters (Great Britain) gold, Heide Rosendahl (West Germany) silver, Burglinde Pollak (East Germany) bronze.

Right: Russian women dominated the 1980 pentathlon, collecting all three medals. Nadyezda Tkachenko is on her way to victory.

MODERN PENTATHLON

In 1912 Baron Pierre de Coubertin, the founder of the modern Games, personally pressed for the inclusion of a new sport to find the perfectly balanced athlete. Legend has it that the event sprang from the following tale: a messenger rides on horseback taking orders to his general; when his horse is killed he fights the enemy with his sword, and with his pistol; he has then to swim a river and run to deliver his message. Riding, fencing, shooting, swimming and cross-country running thus make up the modern pentathlon. A day is allocated to each event.

De Coubertin's wishes were fulfilled in Stockholm, where the inaugural competition was won by Gustaf Lilliehöök, the first of five successive Olympic champions from Sweden.

More recently the modern pentathlon was the centre of Olympic scandal. At Montreal, Boris Onischenko, a competitor of genuine quality, was found guilty of cheating and sent home in disgrace. The Russian's epée had been adjusted to register hits even when the sword had not made contact with his opponent. Four years earlier, Onischenko had won the silver medal.

Far right: Boris Onischenko's Olympic credentials included a gold and two silver medals. Here he shows his paces in the 4000 metres cross-country stage. But Onischenko's successes are now heavily overshadowed by his ban for cheating during the fencing competition in Montreal when his epée was tampered with.

Right and below right: Kathy Taylor of Great Britain shooting and swimming. The shooting competition is pistol expertise on a 25 metre range; swimming is contested over 300 metres freestyle.

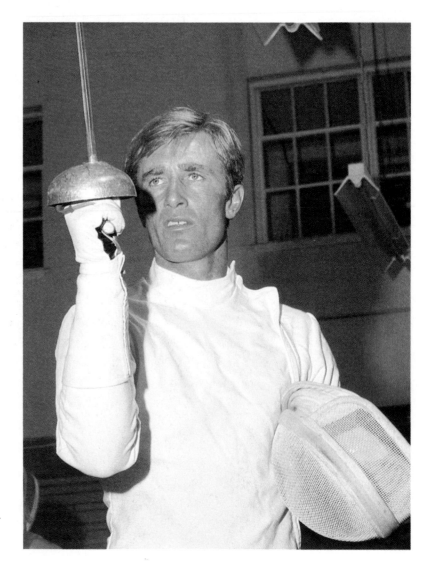

Right: Swordsmanship is part of the craft of the modern pentathlete. Jim Fox, a key member of Great Britain's victory in the 1976 team event, salutes with his epée.
In 1912 George — later General — Patton finished fifth.

WOMEN'S GYMNASTICS

From starting as a sport which initially baffled those who watched it, and even those who reported on it, gymnastics – particularly as displayed by women – has burgeoned into world-wide popularity. The Olympic competition has been responsible for much of the growth. A succession of appealing and charismatic girls have brought to the gymnastics events not just marvellous agility, but also balletic grace sprinkled with a delicate charm.

Vera Caslavska from Czechoslovakia was among the first to capture the hearts of millions following the broadcasting of Games on television. From 1960 to 1968 she produced one entrancing performance after another to win seven gold and four silver medals. Before announcing her retirement in Mexico City, she vastly improved morale in her own country, beating the Russian gymnasts not long after Russia had invaded Czechoslovakia. While still in Mexico City, she married team-mate Josef Odlozil, who had won a silver medal in the 1964 1500 metres.

There were women's team championships (but no individual championships) in 1928, 1936 and 1948. The individual combined exercises plus the four separate exercises – asymmetrical bars, balance beam, floor exercises and vault – were inaugurated in 1952.

1

Above: The Russian women have won every gold medal in the team event since 1952. Olga Korbut (second from the left) was a most popular winner in 1972 and 1976.

Right: The horizontal approach to the vaulting horse. Very impressive height off the floor and the eyes full of concentration for the contact with the horse.

The arrival of Olga Korbut on the Olympic scene brought a tiny, elfin-like gymnast even more loved than Caslavska. At Munich the 17-year old Russian delighted the crowds by winning three golds. Yet she owed her real popularity to a mistake on the asymmetrical bars; as her tears flowed the world cried with – and for – her.

Korbut was superceded at Montreal by Nadia Comaneci from Rumania, who at 14 years of age took the sport by storm. Comaneci became the first Olympic gymnast to score a maximum 10.00; she achieved the perfect mark initially on the asymmetrical bars and followed with six more 10.00s in the rest of the competition. Gymnastics is now the sport of the young; the oldest woman gold medallist, 35-year old Hungarian Agnes Keleti in 1956, seems likely to retain that record for all time. Keleti collected ten medals altogether, all of them after her 30th birthday.

Above: The beautiful co-ordination of Russia's Nelli Kim on the asymmetrical bars.
Right: Nadia Comaneci apparently defying the laws of gravity in the floor exercises.

Far right: Olga Korbut's piece de resistance, a backward somersault on the beam which had never been seen before and was regarded, in some official quarters, as too dangerous.

Women's Gymnastics

The perfection of Comaneci's technique was sometimes dulled by a lack of personal expression; the same could not be said of Nelli Kim whose personality sparkled during competition. Kim and Korbut both retired young as a new influx of small teenage gymnasts came into the arena. Larissa Latynina, another Russian, has set quite a target for the next generation; her total of 18 Olympic medals between 1956 and 1964 included nine golds. In the Soviet Union there are more than 700,000 registered gymnasts so it is no surprise that in the entire Olympic competition the Russians have won more than twice as many medals as Japan, the second most successful nation in gymnastics. In 1980 they provided new champions. Nineteen year old Elena Davydova won the individual combined exercises; another 19-year old Natalya Shaposhnikova triumphed in the vault.

Right: The brilliant Russian Natalya Shaposhnikova at work on the beam. It is an activity which puts tremendous stress on the ankles as the strapping shows.

Right: The athleticism and balletic appeal of women's gymnastics which has attracted the imagination of the public. The asymmetrical bars is one of the four exercises in the women's competition. Medals are at stake in both individual and team events.

Above: On the horse, Elena Davydova, another of the seemingly inexhaustible supply of supremely gifted Russian gymnasts, and a winner in Moscow.

MEN'S GYMNASTICS

The Men's gymnastic competition is staged over six events – floor exercises, parallel bars, pommel horse, rings, horizontal bar and horse vault. Individual medals can be won in each discipline but there is also the team event and the individual combined exercises; overall there are eight events.

Gymnastics has evolved into its present form from circus origins; rope climbing, club swinging and tumbling have been on the list of Olympic sports at one time or another. Carl Schuhmann (Germany) and his team-mates were among the first successful gymnasts in the inaugural competition in 1896. Another German, Alfred Schwarzmann, won five medals in Berlin in 1936; in 1952, at the age of 40 he was still sufficiently agile to win a silver on the horizontal bar.

Japan's influence on the tournament increased in the 1960s and 1970s Sawao Kato and Akinori Nakayama enjoying particular success – and their rivalry with the powerful Russian squad remains the key to much of the competition. In the 1983 World Championship the men's team from China beat both the Soviet Union and Japan, and China's current pre-eminence in men's gymnastics adds a new dimension to this sport of power and perfection. East Germany is another formidable gymnastic nation.

Below: Nikolai Andrianov of the Soviet Union in action on the horizontal bar. Andrianov's tally from Munich, Montreal and Moscow was a remarkable 15 medals.

Right: Mikhail Voronin was joint gold medallist on the horizontal bar at Mexico City. The Russian tied with Akinori Nakayama of Japan with 19.550 points.

One impressive feature of the gymnastics competition is the orderliness of its organisation. The six events (four for women) take place at the same time within the same arena. On completion the gymnasts move in unison around the outside of the arena to the next discipline. The multi-event concept requires enormous concentration from the participants; it is quite normal for applause to be directed at one gymnast while five others are in the middle of their programme on different apparatus.

Judging is based on correctness of execution, difficulty of execution and general aesthetic appeal; continuity of movement, balance, poise and co-ordination are also factors in achieving a high score. The judging has been vulnerable to criticism of political bias, and certainly the more recent trend towards giving the perfect mark of 10.00 has not made the task of the judges any easier.

Every year gymnastics is becoming more skilful, more challenging and more exciting, yet it still retains the essential quality which prompted the Ancient Greeks to elevate it from a sport to an art.

Right: The rings provide a gymnastic test which provokes great admiration from spectators. On the apparatus the gymnast can gather points for keeping still as well as in shoulder-wrenching exercises.

Right: Li Ning of China. The Chinese have not competed in the Olympics since 1952, but the men's gymnastics team beat both Russia and Japan in the World championships in 1983.

Right: East Germany's Michael Nikolay tackling the exercises on the pommel horse. Each discipline contains a compulsory and an optional programme.

CYCLING

In the 1984 Los Angeles Games cycling will be staged in a brand new velodrome, sited between the Coliseum and the yachting centre at Long Beach. It is not unusual for the cyclists to benefit from an Olympic building programme; Tokyo and Moscow, among others, created magnificent arenas and even back in 1908 London's White City provided a special construction.
France, so deeply steeped in the sport, has been particularly successful in Olympic competition, even though Jacques Anquetil, a mighty performer in the professional Tour de France, could not win a medal in his only Olympic appearance at Helsinki in 1952. Patrick Sercu, however, Belgium's six day race specialist, was victorious in the 1000 metres time trial in Tokyo.
The nature of the present competition embraces both sprinting and endurance, from the 1000 metres sprint (with the last 200 metres timed) and 1000 metres time trial, to the 100 kilometre road team time trial and the individual road race which in 1980 in Moscow took place over a 189 kilometre course.

Above: The charm of the countryside setting is in stark contrast to the efforts of the cyclists out on the road where the individual road race usually lasts more than four hours.

Left: The exhilaration of the mass start where one slip can ruin years of Olympic preparation.
Right: The concentration of the sprint finish on the track, often after a version of cat and mouse on wheels. In the sprint events riders often come to a virtual standstill in a battle of minds as well as legs.

Above: Olympic cycling has often been boosted by marvellous new facilities — like this velodrome built for the 1972 Munich Games.

Other forms of Olympic cycling competition are pursuit racing, both team and individual – where opponents start on opposite sides of the track – and the 2000 metre tandem event.

Olympic cycling – like its professional counterpart – has been open to drug abuse. In the 1960 Rome Games Knud Jensen (Denmark) was taken ill during the 100 kilometre race and later died. An illegal stimulant was discovered in his bloodstream.

Right: On a crowded track, cycling is as much a matter of tactics as of technique. Slipstreaming is the subtle art of keeping apace with slightly less effort.

Far right: Wheel to wheel! There are often only centimetres in the outcome in top class cycling, the blurring picture of a sprint finish.

SWIMMING

The greatest single domination of one Olympic sport took place in the Munich pool in 1972. In seven finals Mark Spitz of the United States plunged into the water. Seven times he emerged as a winner with four individual and three team golds.

Spitz stands supreme at the head a long list of distinguished participants in the water sports of swimming, diving and water polo. He had the benefit of the now standardised 50 metre pool. The early Olympic swimmers were not so fortunate; at the inaugural modern Games the competition took place in the sea at Piraeus. Four years later the venue was the River Seine. When a pool was constructed in 1908 in London, it was a vast affair 100 metres long in the centre of the White City athletics track. Though the first champion was a Hungarian, Alfred Hajos, the American influence has always been strong in the water. Johnny Weismuller's popularity and physique led to the film starring Hollywood role of Tarzan after five gold medals in 1924 and 1928. Duke Kahanamoku, from Hawaii, a contemporary of Weismuller's, also turned to acting. His first gold medal in the 100 metres free-style only came after he'd missed a hastily arranged semi-final and won a time trial to qualify for the final; such chaos was unusual in the improved organisation of the Stockholm Olympic Games of 1912.

Below: When Mark Spitz was swimming at Munich in 1972 the demand for seats was enormous; for these spectators, standing-room only.

Right: An inventive look at the Munich swimming-pool which will always be remembered as the venue for Spitz's seven gold medals.

Swimming

In 1984 there will be an Olympic event for synchronised swimming, the gymnastics of the water. Indeed the make-up of the swimming events has changed considerably over the years. Long forgotten now are the 200 metres obstacle race which took place in 1900 and the 1904 plunge for distance! The sidestroke was an early technique; backstroke, breaststoke and freestyle have been long-established methods of racing; butterfly as a separate event was not introduced until 1956.

The first women's swimming events were staged in 1912 at Stockholm; the first champion was an Australian girl, Fanny Durack. Another Australian, Dawn Fraser made Olympic history with three consecutive victories in the 100 metres freestyle in 1956, 1960 and 1964 – a record that remains unequalled in swimming. Kornelia Ender of East Germany left an indelible mark on the 1976 Games with four gold-medal winning performances. Moreover East Germany won 11 of the 15 events in the women's competition at Montreal. In 1980 Barbara Krause proved a worthy successor to Ender and East Germany collected another 12 golds.

Left: Sixteen year old Debbie Meyer became the first swimmer to win three individual races in one Olympic Games. She triumphed in the 200, 400 and 800 metres freestyle at Mexico City in 1968. Below: Dawn Fraser defied asthma to become an Olympic legend. Her feat in winning the same swimming event, the 100 metres freestyle, in three successive Olympic Games is unparalleled. Right: With the importance of fractions of seconds determining a gold medal, a good start is vital.

Swimming

Much of the early controversy in the judging of swimming has been eliminated by the sophistication of electronic timing. At Munich, for example, the naked eye could not possibly have separated Gunnar Larsson (Sweden) and Tim McKee (United States) at the end of the final of the 400 metres individual medley. The timing mechanism awarded Larsson the gold by two thousandths of a second! Even in 1960 disputes were still happening, notably when John Devitt (Australia) congratulated Lance Larson (United States) after a close finish in the 100 metres freestyle final; to Devitt's astonishment he found that the judges had awarded the race to him and placed Larson second.

For Larson the pain of an unfair defeat; but Dick Roth another American was prepared to endure the physical agony of appendicitis to win his gold at Tokyo in 1964. Roth had to be fed intravenously but still triumphed in the 400 metres individual medley race; only then did he consent to the operation.

Overall in swimming the United States has 296 medals, far ahead of Australia with 89. Agnieszka Czopek's third place in the women's 400 metres individual medley in 1980 won Poland's first ever swimming medal.

Below: Swimming's mightiest Olympian, Mark Spitz. Spitz had been widely fancied to bring in a shoal of medals at Mexico City; in Munich he did not disappoint.

Right: The warm water of the modern 50 metres pool is a more conducive setting for Olympic swimming than the sea off Athens or the River Seine, the first two venues in the Games.

An Austrian representing Italy has set the highest standards in the men's highboard diving competion. Klaus Dibiasi warmed up for a memorable sequence by winning a silver medal as a 17-year old at Tokyo. At the next *three* Games he was Olympic champion, with a second place in the springboard event at Mexico City for good measure. Men's diving became part of the Games in 1904, women's eight years later. In 1936 Majorie Gestring (United States) became springboard champion at the remarkably young age of 13. In 1952 and 1956 Pat McCormick also from the United States won both highboard and springboard golds.

Mexico's Joaquim Capilla Perez gave perfect evidence of his improvement in the men's highboard competition by progressing from bronze in 1948 to silver in 1952 and gold at Melbourne in 1956.

The diving programme consists of compulsory and voluntary dives. The marks for the quality of the dives are computed with the tariff or the value of the degree of difficulty to produce the final score for each competitor.

Right: The United States team beats East Germany in the 4 × 100 metres freestyle relay. The result was the same in 1968, 1972 and 1976. In America's absence from Moscow, East Germany did win in 1980.

Below: Shane Gould (Australia) won the 200 and 400 metres freestyle and the 200 metres individual medley, all in world record times at Munich.

Above right: Kornelia Ender (East Germany) retired and married Roland Matthes, a fellow East German Olympic champion after her four golds in 1976.

DIVING AND WATER POLO

International diving tables classify each dive by its direction and the body position of the diver. Directions are either forward, back, reverse, inward, twist or armstand (handstand at the outset). Body positions are straight, piked, tucked or free.

The Olympic water polo competition began in 1900 and apart from the interim Games of 1906 has been present on the list since. Hungary has been the predominant nation with six victories. Oliver Halasy, a member of the winning teams in 1932 and 1936 and runner-up in 1928, set another example of Olympic heroism. Halasy, who in all played in 96 internationals for Hungary, became a top-class sportsman despite losing a foot in a childhood accident.

Hungary, in fact, have not been out of the water polo medals in the last twelve Games. Johnny Weismuller was one of a number of Olympic swimming champions who also used his talents in water polo. With Weismuller the Americans finished third in 1924 as they did eight years later when Duke Kahanamoku was still looking for Olympic medals as a squad member at the age of 41.

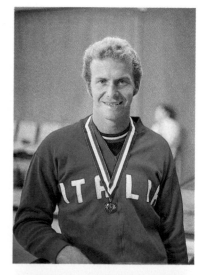

Above right: Klaus Dibiasi was born in Austria of Italian parentage. After his silver medal at Tokyo, local supporters in Bolzano in Italy built him his own diving tank. Dibiasi showed his gratitude with three consecutive highboard gold medals.
Right: Ulrika Knape (Sweden) won the 1972 women's highboard title and took the silver in the springboard.

Below: Olympic water polo has been dominated by Hungary. Not since 1924 have the Hungarians failed to win a medal. In 1904 club teams from the United States won all three medals.

Left: Olympic diving is a mixture of dramatic acrobatics, concentration and elegance. Above all the diver needs courage; one mistake can mean a very painful landing in the water at some 30 miles per hour.

Overleaf: The amazing grace of a world diving champion, Wendy Wyland (United States).

EQUESTRIAN EVENTS

For elegance and sophistication, the equestrian events still rate highly in the Olympic Games. The combination of dressage and showjumping requires dignity and discipline; the three-day event remains a searching examination for horse and rider.

To meet Olympic standards horses often need at least five years training for grand prix dressage, a catalogue of classical exercises – an elevated slow trot (passage), an elevated marking-time at the trot (piaffe), canter changes of leg at every stride, changes of direction on two trots at the canter, and pirouette. As well as individual team events, dressage forms the first stage of the three-day event.

In the Olympic arena Henri St. Cyr mastered the dressage discipline, gold medallist in the individual competition in 1952 and 1956, and in the Swedish team success in the same years. Only antiquated rules, which were immediately changed, had robbed St. Cyr of another gold in 1948. Sweden won comfortably enough but were then disqualified because one of their team was not a commissioned officer. Equestrianism emerged from a staunch military background.

Below: Dressage where the horse and the rider must move as one. Its origins come from the great riding schools of France, Germany and Austria. The requirements of a dressage horse are a calm temperament, intelligence and elegance.

Right: The 1972 equestrian events attracted vast crowds to Munich's Olympic stadium.

Equestrian Events

In 1956 the equestrian sports were separated from the main Games. When the hub of the XVIth Olympiad was at Melbourne in November and December, the equestrian medals had already been decided in Stockholm the previous June. Australia's quarantine laws did not allow easy entry to the animals.

The cross-country stretch in the three-day event is regarded as the central stage, and receives higher priority than dressage and show jumping in the computing of the scores. Great Britain's winning squad in 1968 contained 54-year old Major Derek Allhusen. It also included Jane Bullen, the first woman to win a team gold medal in this competition.

Showjumping is the oldest equestrian sport in the Games, introduced in 1900 when the Belgian, Aime Haegeman on Benton II won the inaugural competition. The present competition allows for four riders from each nation, with the best three scoring. For the XXIII Olympiad in Los Angeles, the site for the equestrian events is at Santa Anita.

Below: The hazards of the cross-country stage of the three-day event. As this competitor in the Munich Games attempts to avoid disaster, his horse manages to keep at least his ears above water!

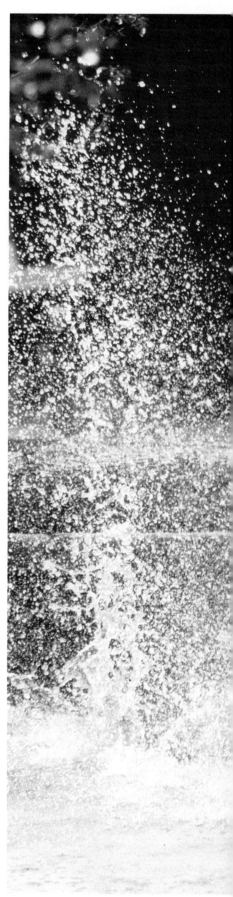

Left: The water obstacles often provide the greatest drama in the cross-country section of the three-day event. Time is an opponent as well as the course.

Overleaf: The exceptional style of Hans-Gunther Winkler of West Germany. Winkler collected five show jumping gold medals, and in 1976, at the age of 50, added a silver to his tally.

FENCING

In Moscow in 1980, twenty-one year old Vladimir Lapitsky was rushed on a stretcher from the fencing hall after being run through – in a complete accident – by a broken blade. This happened in his contest against Adam Robak of Poland in the men's team foil competition. The young Russian survived, but the episode served as a reminder of the risks involved in fencing. Fencing has been a continuous thread throughout the history of the modern Games. The established formula now is individual and team competitions for men in foil, epée and sabre; women are restricted to the foil, again in team and individual contests. Edoardo Mangiarotti's supreme skills brought him 13 medals between 1936 and 1960, after being converted to left-handed fencing by his father. Aladar Gerevich (Hungary) totalled one individual and six team gold medals in the sabre over the same period.

Electronic apparatus has greatly assisted in the scoring of hits in foil and epée, but the sabre – where the cutting edge, as well as the point of the weapon, scores valid touches – is not so adaptable. Instead the hits are awarded by a panel of judges.

Below: The electronic complexities that make the awarding of hits in foil and epée so much easier. The shining of the white lights records contact on a non-valid surface like the hands, arms, legs or mask.

Above: Olympic fencing, the sport which has evolved from duelling with swords, once the social convention for settling disputes between two gentlemen.

Left: The mask does not count as a valid zone for hits in the foil event — but it does for both the epée and sabre competitions.

ARCHERY

Eighteen year old John Williams, a soldier in the US Army, took the glory when archery returned to the Olympic Games at Munich in 1972 after an absence of 52 years. Williams belied his youth with a superb display of calmness and added a world record to go with his gold medal. Forty-two year old Doreen Wilber, also from the United States, was the women's champion.

The sophisticated equipment of archery in the present day is very different from the style in the early days of Olympic competition. Women, rare Olympians at the turn of the century, took part in 1904, though in St. Louis there were only American entrants.

The popularity of archery as an Olympic sport fizzled out after the 1920 games in Antwerp. The Belgians insisted on conducting the competition with their own regulations; only three nations – Belgium, Holland and France – competed, and not surprisingly the tournament was not re-instated for 1924.

Archery today is a detailed test of marksmanship. To win his gold medal Williams had to fire 288 arrows – 72 each at distances of 30, 50, 70 and 90 metres. With one arrow he totally missed the target. For women the ranges are 30, 50, 60 and 70 metres.

Below: Olympic archery is an immense test of nerve under the pressure of international competition. Few sports have such a small margin of error.

Right: Archers compete side-by-side with equipment which is a far cry from the weapons of medieval bowmen. Concentration is essential for success with 2 rounds, of 144 arrows each, to be fired.

RIFLE AND PISTOL SHOOTING

In 1900 there was *live* pigeon shooting on the Olympic agenda. But the style of competition and the weapons used have changed many times since then. In 1980 the shooting format contained free pistol, rapid fire pistol, three-position small-bore rifle (prone, kneeling and standing), small-bore rifle (prone), skeet shooting, Olympic trap shooting and running game target. In the 1984 Olympic Games there will be an air-rifle event as well. Women first competed alongside the men in 1968, and in 1976 Margaret Murdock of the USA outshot a field of men to finish second in the three-position small-bore rifle. An innovation at Los Angeles is three specific events for women; air-rifle, pistol and small-bore rifle.

Marksmen and women are less vulnerable to age than some Olympic sportsmen. Oscar Swahn of Sweden won a silver medal in the team running deer event in 1920 at the age of 72! Eight years earlier he'd collected the last of his three gold medals; his son also won three shooting gold medals in 1908 and 1912.

Right: Today's pistol competitors have a perfect example in the dedication of Karoly Takacs from Hungary, who was a right-handed European champion in the 1930s until an army accident. Takacs became a left-handed Olympic champion in 1948 and 1952.

Below: So high are the standards in the Olympic shooting competition that near maximum scores are essential for any medal hopes.

Right: There are two events in small-bore rifle shooting, the three-positions (prone, kneeling and standing) and prone.

BASKETBALL

One of the truly unforgettable moments in Olympic history occurred on the basketball court at the Munich Olympics in 1972. The United States – unbeaten in 63 Olympic matches since the inclusion of basketball in the Games in 1936 (a run that brought seven consecutive gold medals) – led the Soviet Union 50-49 with three seconds remaining. After the hiatus of a controversial restart, Alexander Belov smuggled the ball into the American basket inside those seconds, and the Americans, despite frantic protests, were beaten at last.

The Soviet Union is set to establish a similar domination in the women's event. The Russian girls won the first two tournaments, in 1976 and 1980, inspired by the huge Iuliana Semenova, seven feet tall, more than 280lbs in weight and wearing size 18 shoes! To participate in the finals, countries must submit their basketball squad for qualifying competitions. In 1976 and 1980 the medals were disputed by twelve men's teams and six women's. In the absence of the United States in Moscow the men's gold medal went to the world champions Yugoslavia, who beat Italy 86-77.

Right: Action from the explosive 1972 men's basketball final. The United States lost their unbeaten record and the gold medal in the last second and did not attend the ceremony to collect their silver.

Right: The popularity of basketball in the United States has created an Olympic domination. Apart from their much-chronicled defeat by the USSR in 1972, and their boycott in 1980, the Americans have won every men's tournament.

Right: Japan versus Czechoslovakia in Olympic competition. The inaugural women's basketball tournament was staged in Montreal in 1976 and like many of the new women's events was a great success.

FOOTBALL

In 1980 the Olympic football tournament comprised 32 matches; two million people attended the competition, swelling vastly the overall attendance at the Moscow Games.

Football thus recaptured a prominence lost since before World War II; in Paris in 1924 the game's appeal contributed more than a third of the total Olympic revenue. More than most events it has suffered because of the lack of definition of the status of its participants. Eastern European countries have consistently fielded players called "amateurs" who have in reality been full-time performers in their domestic leagues. The 1980 final, between Czechoslovakia and East Germany, reinforced the point. Not since 1948 has a Western nation won the football gold medal. That went to Sweden, whose famous Gre-No-Li trio, Gunnar Gren, Gunnar Nordahl and Nils Liedholm, all later enjoyed superb professional careers. Nordahl in fact participated in one of the most unusual goals in Olympic football history. In the semi-final, against Denmark, he found himself in an offside position as Sweden attacked. He stepped into the net and actually caught the scoring header from Carlsson; technically out of play, Nordahl's quick-thinking allowed the goal to stand.

Below: Czechoslovakia, in white, on their way to Olympic gold in Moscow, beating East Germany 1-0 with a late goal from a substitute, Svoboda.

Right: The Lenin stadium in Moscow had a vast crowd for the 1980 football final, despite the USSR's semi-final defeat.

VOLLEYBALL

Volleyball, so popular in Japan, appropriately made its first appearance in the Games in Tokyo in 1964. Competitions for men and women were introduced, and the local girls were rewarded for extreme single-mindedness and dedication, even by Olympic standards! Japan's squad sacrificed the other facets of their lives for 18 months, during which they did nothing except prepare for the Olympic tournament. When they beat Russia in the final, the host nation went wild with delight.

Japan's men have also had their share of success, triumphant in Munich, but the predominant nation in both competitions has been the Soviet Union; only once have their teams failed to reach the final. The Russian men and women have lost only six times between them in the five Games since volleyball has been incorporated into the list of Olympic sports.

The game itself has established a deserved place in the Olympic schedule by providing a fast-moving spectacle.

Right: Cuba in action in the 1980 Olympic volleyball tournament. The gold medals in both men's and women's competition once again went to the USSR, who dominate the sport.

Below: The fast-moving six-a-side spectacle of volleyball. Matches are of three or five sets; points can only be scored by the serving team, and a set lasts until one team scores 15 points with a two-point lead.

HOCKEY

If much of Olympic sport has fallen under the domination of the
Soviet Union and the United States, the hockey competition still
offers hope for success for India and Pakistan. India, indeed, is
the super-power of the men's game, their subtle play characterised
by deft stick-handling and agile running. From 1928 to 1956
inclusive the Indians were invincible, and their victory in
Moscow – a 4-3 win over Spain in the final – took their tally of
gold medals to eight.

Four years earlier New Zealand and Australia had taken gold and
silver respectively with India's advantage of natural talent
somewhat nullified by Montreal's artificial surface.

Field hockey has always been a sport for women as well, but it was
not recognised by the Olympics until the 1980 Games. The
tournament provided a memorable landmark for a new nation.
Zimbabwe (formerly Rhodesia) were the first ladies Olympic
hockey champions. The men from Tanzania were less fortunate
conceding 54 goals in five games, including an 18-0 loss to India;
yet their long-suffering goalkeeper Leopold Gracias emerged as
one of the real characters of the Games.

A far closer contest took place in Mexico in 1968. Holland beat
Spain 1-0 but it took until the sixth period of extra time to find the
decisive goal, a total playing time of 2 hours 25 minutes.

*Right: West Germany won the
hockey gold in 1972 beating
Pakistan in the final. The host
country's team built its success on
the foundation of a solid defence
which kept out more talented
opposition.*

Left: India had to come from behind to beat Spain in the 1980 final. Their eventual 4-3 victory re-affirmed their domination of Olympic hockey; it provided India's eighth gold medal. From 1928 to 1956 they were invincible.

Below: A triumph for a new nation in a new sport. The first women's Olympic hockey tournament, in Moscow, was won by Zimbabwe, formerly known as Rhodesia.

HANDBALL

Before 1972 handball had only once been part of the Olympics. That was in Berlin in 1936, when it was staged as an outdoor eleven-a-side game, with Germany winning on home soil. When the Games returned to West Germany 36 years later handball was back, but the formula now was seven-a-side on an indoor court. In 1976 the women's handball competition was introduced.

In many areas of Europe it has grown into a very popular indoor sport, although remaining virtually unknown in other parts of the world. The 1980 Moscow men's final was one of the highlights of the entire Games when East Germany defeated the Russian favourites 23 goals to 22 after extra time. Amongst the gold medallists was Hans-Georg Beyer, a 23-year old motor mechanic in the army who extended a marvellous family involvement in Olympic sport. Brother, Udo, was the 1976 shot put champion; sister Gisela just finished out of the medals in the 1980 discus. The Soviet Union have triumphed in both women's competitions, and in its present form handball has given all its medals to eastern European nations.

Right: Men's handball has provided three different winners since it was introduced as an indoor sport in 1972. Yugoslavia won the inaugural tournament. Russia succeeded in 1976, East Germany in 1980.

Below: Yugoslavia versus the People's Republic of Congo in the 1980 women's handball competition. Yugoslavia achieved a massive 39-9 victory, and went on to win the silver medal.

BOXING

The boxing tournament has developed into a substantial section of the Games since the sport was first introduced in 1904. Then there were seven weight divisions and a clean sweep for the United States.

For Los Angeles a new class has been created, super heavyweight. Yet at the last three Olympiads the heavyweight division has had its own "super" boxer. Cuba's Teofilo Stevenson punched his way to three successive Olympic titles; during that eight-year span he refused multi-million dollar offers to turn professional. Laszlo Papp of Hungary – middleweight champion in 1948 and light middleweight champion in 1952 and 1956 – is the only other Olympic fighter to achieve that feat.

The Olympic ring has been a great training ground for later world professional champions, like Cassius Clay, George Foreman, and Joe Frazier. The brothers Leon and Michael Spinks both won golds at Montreal and graduated to world titles. Floyd Patterson was an Olympic champion at 17, while Ingemar Johannsson who later beat Patterson for the world heavyweight title was disqualified in the 1952 Olympic heavyweight final for "inactivity"; he only received his silver medal 30 years later.

Below: Muhammed Ali, then known as Cassius Clay, first came to prominence in Rome in 1960 when he won the light heavyweight division.

Right: If Ali became "The Greatest", arguably the greatest Olympic boxer has been Teofilo Stevenson of Cuba (right), heavyweight supreme.

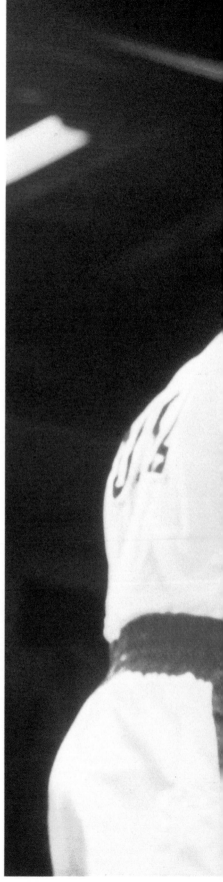

JUDO

Judo arrived on the Olympic scene in 1964 and immediately produced a shock result. In their own Budokan Hall in Tokyo the Japanese were expected to be unbeatable; indeed they did collect three of the four golds.

The prestige event, however, the open class, was won by a Dutchman, Anton Geesink, who had sharpened his craft by training in Japan and outmanoeuvred the local favourite Akio Kaminaga.

The Mexico Games did not include judo but the sport returned in 1972. By 1980 it had extended to eight categories. In 1972 no silver medal was awarded in the up to 63kg division; the runner-up Bakhaavaa Buidaa, representing Mongolia, was eliminated after a dope test had found positive results.

Fears that the Japanese would dominate the competition have proved groundless; twenty-three different nations have collected medals. Angelo Parisi has been successful for two different countries. Born in Italy, he won a bronze for Great Britain in Munich. Eight years later he had taken French citizenship and for his new country gathered gold and silver in Moscow.

Below and right: The drama of Olympic judo. The object in this sport, based on an art of self-defence, is to throw one's opponent and immobilize him for up to 30 seconds, or to achieve a submission by an armlock or stranglehold. Judo was introduced into the Olympics in 1964 and is now firmly part of the showcase of the Games.

WEIGHTLIFTING

The musclemen of weightlifting were part of the Olympic movement at its re-birth in 1896. The present day competition format comprising two lifts, the snatch and the clean and the jerk, has evolved from a variety of past events, including one-hand lifting.

In the snatch the bar must be lifted in a single movement from the ground to above the head with the arms fully extended. The clean and jerk is a two-stage lift with the bar being held at shoulder level before being 'jerked' overhead. As man has grown bigger as a species the weights lifted have regularly increased. The competitors are now divided into ten weight categories.

As in boxing it's the big men who have brought the most charisma to weightlifting, notably Vasili Alexeev, the enormous Russian who reigned supreme on the world and Olympic stage from 1970 to 1977. Harald Sakata from the United States, a silver medallist in 1948, found fame on a wider scale when he played a leading part in the James Bond film *Goldfinger*. Records reveal a remarkable age difference in competitors; Teunist Jonck of South Africa was 56 when he lifted in 1952; Djemal from Turkey competed at 13 years of age in Paris in 1924.

Below: Muhammed Manzoor in the 56kg class at Montreal.

Right: The mighty Alexeev. A 15lb baby, his weight approached 350lbs at his lifting peak. He was never coached and often trained in the middle of the night. For relaxation he loved the music of the Welsh singer, Tom Jones.

WRESTLING

The first records of wrestling in the Olympic programme can be found in the documentation of the Ancient Games. In 708 BC it was included both as a separate event and as part of the pentathlon. Free-style wrestling was incorporated into the Modern Games in the IIIrd Olympiad in St. Louis in 1904.
Each contest is of three, three-minute rounds, and the outcome – decided by officials at the end of the bout – is by disqualification for three cautions, or when a fall is scored. A fall is defined when both shoulders of the wrestler are held in contact with the mat for what is known as a "one-count".
Among the great freestylers was Aleksandr Medved of the Soviet Union who made history with consecutive gold medals in the competitions for light heavyweight in 1964, heavyweight in 1968 and superheavyweight in 1972. Medved was comparatively small weighing some 230lbs and often beat wrestlers more than 100lbs heavier than himself.
In 1948 a delighted Turkish government lavished money on victorious team of wrestlers – thereby rendering them ineligible to take part in future Olympic Games!

Right: The struggle for supremacy in the freestyle wrestling mat.

Below: Switzerland's Jimmy Martinetti in action in the middleweight division. The wrestling takes place on an octagonal mat 12 metres in diameter. Three concentric circles define the area for competition.

Wrestling

Greco-Roman wrestling differs from freestyle in that the competitors are not allowed to use their legs in the various holds. Carl Westergren of Sweden, famous for the 'Westergren roll', was arguably the doyen of Greco-Roman wrestlers, competing in four Olympics; his roll of honour contains gold medals as a middleweight in 1920 and 1924 and as a heavyweight in 1932. Another Swede, Ivar Johansson, combined two Greco-Roman victories in 1932 and 1936 with the middleweight freestyle championship at the 1932 Los Angeles Games.

Greco-Roman wrestling was one of the nine sports in the initial Modern Games programme in Athens in 1896. Then it was not just a contest for specialists. Carl Schuhmann of Germany had won three gold medals for gymnastics when he became the first Olympic champion; Schuhmann remarkably stood only 5ft 4ins tall. On his path to the final he overcame Great Britain's weightlifting champion Launceston Eliot. With no time limits to bouts at that time the final took two days to decide!

Right: Greco-Roman wrestling comprised ten weight categories in 1980. Sweden has won most gold medals with 19, followed by Finland with 18 and Hungary 12. Russian wrestlers have won the most medals overall in this event — with 57.

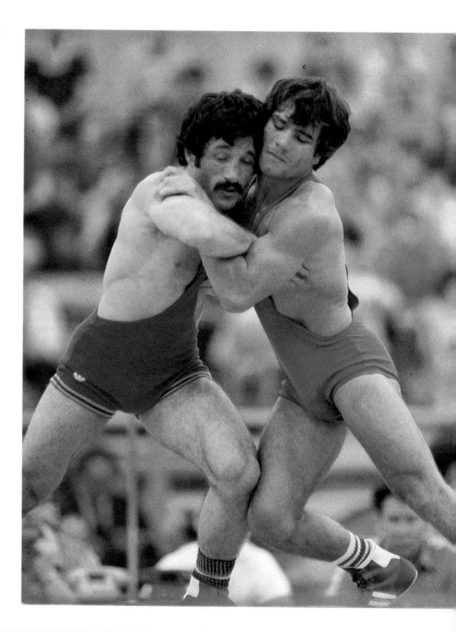

Right: A bout in the 1980 bantamweight division of Greco-Roman wrestling between Mihai Botila of Rumania who finished fourth, and the Italian Antonino Caltabiano who, in the final placings, came fifth.

If at times a somewhat remote Olympic sport, because so often it is staged away from the main Games' centre, yachting has been a thread running throughout the competition since 1896 – though rough seas did lead to its cancellation in that first year.

Change has occurred often in the classes of competition; indeed the IOC decreed in 1922 that only the one-man dinghy (the Finn since 1952) is to be a constant. Other types of craft have come in and gone out of fashion. In 1980 at the Estonian venue of Tallin, contests took place in Finn, 470, Tornado, Star, Flying Dutchman and Soling.

Paul Elvstrom (Denmark) showed the value to his rivals of personal physical fitness in a supreme showing of four consecutive dinghy victories from 1948 to 1960. Women were accepted in competitions long before their participation in track and field, and in 1908 Frances Clytie Rivett-Carnac (Great Britain) and her husband took the gold medal in the 7-metre class.

Above: Water-proofing protection coupled with freedom for movement, essentials for the garb of the Olympic yachtsman.

Left: The catamaran class of international Tornado was introduced at Montreal. The first winners were the British crew of Reg White and John Osborn. In 1980 Brazil provided the Olympic champions with Denmark second, and Sweden third.

Above: The crew of this Flying Dutchman suspended above the water. Olympic yachting is decided on the six fastest times of each vessel from seven races.

Left: The only three-man crew in present Olympic competition is in the Soling class, where Denmark showed their expertise on water with wins in 1976 and 1980.

Right: The marvellous sight of Olympic yachts at full tilt with spinakers billowing. The majesty belies the rivalry which is just as immense as in any other event in the Games. Its press and television coverage is often less, because by necessity, the course — like this at Kiel in 1972 — is often far from the centre of the Games.

CANOEING

Two types of canoes are raced in the Olympics, the kayak (of Eskimo origin) and the Canadian canoe (developed by Red Indians). Events are held for men in singles, pairs and fours over 500 metres and 1,000 metres; the women's competition is restricted to kayaks. A new race, the women's Kayak (Fours) 500 metres has been added to the 1984 programme. Most recent venues have been man-made courses of flat, still water. The 10,000 metres endurance races have been discontinued since 1956. Gert Fredriksson of Sweden gathered in the remarkable haul of six gold medals between 1948 and 1960; he was 40 when he won the kayak pairs with Sven-Olaf Sjodelius in Rome, and would have been even more successful but for World War II.

Germany asked the IOC to introduce canoeing as an Olympic sport into the Berlin Games in 1936. When the Games returned to West Germany 36 years later, eleven canoeing events were held with three slalom races for men and one for women. Because of difficulties of providing a worthy course there have been no slalom competitions since then.

Right: The Canadian canoe differs from the kayak in shape and in the paddle design. The first gold medal in a Canadian canoe race went appropriately to Canada's Francis Amyot in 1936.

Below: The drama of the only Olympic slalom competition staged in Munich in 1972. The 'wildwater' test for the competitors was to steer the kayak through a number of gates.

Right: Kayaks are raced as singles, pairs (as here) and in fours. Much work has gone on in recent years to streamline the canoe and also the paddles.

ROWING

If you are in Los Angeles for the XXIIIrd Olympiad, you will have to travel 84 miles from the Track and Field centre at the Coliseum to the rowing venue at Lake Casitas. It's not quite as central as the River Seine is to Paris, where 84 years ago rowing was given its unofficial baptism as an Olympic sport.

The traditions of Olympic rowing have been handed down from father to son in an unusual number of family successes. Charles Burnell (1908) and his son Richard (1948) were both gold medallists for Great Britain. Paul and Bernard Costello (United States), John senior and John junior Kelly (United States) and Guy senior and Guy junior Nickalls (Great Britain) all won medals. Twin brothers Jorg and Bernd Landvoigt (East Germany) were champions in the coxless pairs in 1976 and in 1980. A full programme of rowing now involves single, double and quadruple sculls, coxed and coxless pairs and fours, and eights. There was no women's rowing until 1976; in Montreal and Moscow six events took place with East Germany by far the most powerful nation.

Left: Single sculling. The course length has now been standardised at 2000 metres for men and 1000 metres for women.

Below: East Germany — represented here by Dahne and Noack — have developed into a formidable force in rowing.
Overleaf: The majestic grace of the Olympic eights competition.

WINDSURFING

The rapid increase in popularity of board-sailing or wind-surfing has been reflected in its first inclusion in the Olympic programme at Los Angeles. Undoubtedly it will create special interest at the Long Beach centre where it will be staged as part of the yachting regatta.

The competition is to be organised on the principles of the yachting events. The boards will be raced around the same course, the Olympic triangle, with each leg of that triangle one mile long. It is estimated that the winning times will be between one and one and a half hours in each race.

In each yachting class there are seven races with each entrant counting his six fastest times for the final placing. For board-sailing, however, there will be twelve such heats; the ten best times for each individual to be computed into the final score. There are already many types of craft, but the initial Olympic competition is restricted to wind-gliders. Local knowledge of wind and water is a great advantage in international competition, but at Los Angeles this will help only one American, because each nation is restricted to one entrant. The favourites for the inaugural medals come from Holland, France, Australia and the United States.

The Swatek sisters from the United States demonstrating that women are also a force in board-sailing. The first Olympic competition will include only one type of craft, the wind-glider with a crew of one.

These records show the Olympic Gold Medal Winner for every event covered in the last 20 years of the Olympic Games. A space has been left in the record table for each event, to allow you to fill in the 1984 Gold Medal Winners in the XXIII Olympic Games in Los Angeles. Where no date appears in these records (from 1964–1984) the event was not held.

PRESIDENTS OF THE INTERNATIONAL OLYMPIC COMMITTEE

1894-1896	Dimitrios Vikelas (Greece)
1896-1925	Baron Pierre de Coubertin (France)
1925-1942	Count Henri de Baillet Latout (Belgiur
1946-1952	Sigfrid Edstrom (Sweden)
1952-1972	Avery Brundage (USA)
1972-1980	Lord Killanin (Ireland)
1980-	H.E. Juan Antonio Samaranch (Spain

Olympiad number	Year	Venue	Date	Competitors Men	Women	Total
I	1896	Athens	6-15 Apr	311	–	311
II	1900	Paris	2-22 Jul	1,319	11	1,330
III	1904	St Louis	1 Jul-23 Nov	617	8	625
IV	1908	London	27 Apr-31 Oct	2,023	36	2,059
V	1912	Stockholm	5 May-22 Jul	2,484	57	2,541
VI	1916	Berlin	Cancelled	–	–	–
VII	1920	Antwerp	14-29 Aug	2,543	63	2,606
VIII	1924	Paris	5-27 Jul	2,956	136	3,092
IX	1928	Amsterdam	28 Jul-12 Aug	2,725	290	3,015
X	1932	Los Angeles	30 Jul-14 Aug	1,281	127	1,408
XI	1936	Berlin	1-16 Aug	3,741	328	4,069
XII	1940	Helsinki	Cancelled	–	–	–
XIII	1944	London	Cancelled	–	–	–
XIV	1948	London	29 Jul-14 Aug	4,304	385	4,689
XV	1952	Helsinki	19 Jul-3 Aug	4,407	518	4,925
XVI	1956	Melbourne†	22 Nov-8 Dec	2,959	384	3,343
XVII	1960	Rome	25 Aug-11 Sep	4,800	537	5,337
XVIII	1964	Tokyo	10-24 Oct	4,826	732	5,558
XIX	1968	Mexico City	12-27 Oct	5,215	844	6,059
XX	1972	Munich	26 Aug-11 Sep	6,086	1,070	7,156
XXI	1976	Montreal	17 Jul-1 Aug	4,834	1,251	6,085
XXII	1980	Moscow	19 July-2 Aug	4,238	1,088	5,326
XXIII	1984	Los Angeles	28 Jul-12 Aug	–	–	–
XXIV	1988	Seoul	–	–	–	–

† Equestrian events were held in Stockholm: the total number of competitors includes 146 men and 13 women who competed there.

ODD SPORTS OUT

Several sports – and many disciplines within each sport – have been adopted and then abandoned from one Olympiad to the next. This is a list of some of the more unusual events that have, at one time or another, attracted athletes to compete for that elusive Olympic Gold Medal

Tug-of-war
Discus Greek-style
Discus-Both hands
Shot-Both hands
Javelin-Both hands
Standing jump-Long jump
Standing jump-High jump
Standing jump-Triple jump

Rope climbing
Throwing the stone
Tumbling
Indian club swinging
Swimming-200m obstacle event

ABBREVIATIONS OF COUNTRIES

Aus	Australia	GDR	German Democratic Republic	Por	Portugal
Aut	Austria	Ger	Germany	PRK	D.P.R. Korea
Bah	Bahamas	Gre	Greece	Rom	Rumania
Bar	Barbados	Neth	Netherlands	SKR	South Korea
Bel	Belgium	Hun	Hungary	Swi	Switzerland
Ber	Bermuda	Ind	India	Swe	Sweden
Bra	Brazil	Irl	Ireland	Czh	Czechoslovakia
Bul	Bulgaria	Irn	Iran	Tha	Thailand
Can	Canada	Ita	Italy	Tri	Trinidad and Tobago
Cub	Cuba	Jam	Jamaica	Tur	Turkey
Den	Denmark	Jpn	Japan	USSR	Soviet Union
Esp	Spain	Ken	Kenya	Uga	Uganda
Eth	Ethiopia	Mex	Mexico	Uru	Uruguay
Fin	Finland	Nor	Norway	USA	United States
Fr	France	NZ	New Zealand	Ven	Venezuela
GB	Great Britain	Pak	Pakistan	Yug	Yugoslavia
		Pol	Poland	Zimb	Zimbabwe

GOLD MEDALS 1964–1984

ARCHERY

Men
1972	J. Williams (USA) 2528pts
1976	D. Pace (USA) 2571pts ●
1980	T. Poikolainen (Fin) 2455pts
1984	....

Women
1972	D. Wilbur (USA) 2424pts
1976	L. Ryon (USA) 2499pts ●
1980	K. Lasaberidze (USSR) 2491pts
1984	....

ASSOCIATION FOOTBALL
1964	Hungary
1968	Hungary
1972	Poland
1976	German Democratic Republic
1980	Czechoslovakia
1984	....

ATHLETICS – MEN

100 Metres
1964	R. Hayes (USA) 10.0sec
1968	J. Hines (USA) 9.95sec ●
1972	V. Borzov (USSR) 10.14sec
1976	H. Crawford (Tri) 10.06sec
1980	A. Wells (GB) 10.25sec
1984	....

* Current World/Olympic record ● Current Olympic reco

200 Metres
1964   H. Carr (USA) 20.3sec
1968   T. Smith (USA) 19.83sec ●
1972   V. Borzov (USSR) 20.0 sec
1976   D. Quarrie (Jam) 20.23sec
1980   P. Mennea (Ita) 20.19 sec
1984 ....

400 Metres
1964   M. Larrabee (USA) 45.1 sec
1968   L. Evans (USA) 43.86 sec*
1972   V. Matthews (USA) 44.66 sec
1976   A. Juantorena (Cub) 44.26 sec
1980   V. Markin (USSR) 44.60 sec
1984 ....

800 Metres
1964   P. Snell (NZ) 1min 45.1sec
1968   R. Doubell (Aus) 1min 44.3sec
1972   D. Wottle (USA) 1min 45.9sec
1976   A. Juantorena (Cub) 1min 43.50sec ●
1980   S. Ovett (GB) 1min 45.4sec
1984 ....

1500 Metres
1964   P. Snell (NZ) 3min 38.1sec
1968   K. Keino (Ken) 3min 34.9sec ●
1972   P. Vasala (Fin) 3min 36.3sec
1976   J. Walker (NZ) 3min 39.2sec
1980   S. Coe (GB) 3min 38.4sec
1984 ....

5000 Metres
1964   B. Schul (USA) 13min 48.8sec
1968   M. Gammoudi (Tun) 14min 05.0sec
1972   L. Viren (Fin) 13min 26.4sec
1976   L. Viren (Fin) 13min 24.76sec
1980   M. Yifter (Eth) 13min 21.0sec
1984 ....

10,000 Metres
1964   B. Mills (USA) 28min 24.4sec
1968   N. Temu (Ken) 29min 27.4sec
1972   L. Viren (Fin) 27min 38.4sec ●
1976   L. Viren (Fin) 27min 40.38sec
1980   M. Yifter (Eth) 27min 42.7sec
1984 ....

Marathon
1964   A. Bikila (Eth) 2hr 12min 11sec
1968   M. Wold (Eth) 2hr 20min 26sec
1972   F. Shorter (USA) 2hr 12min 19sec
1976   W. Cierpinski (GDR) 2hr 09min 55sec ●
1980   W. Cierpinski (GDR) 2hr 11min 03sec
1984 ....

110 Metres Hurdles
1964   H. Jones (USA) 13.6sec
1968   W. Davenport (USA) 13.3sec
1972   R. Milburn (USA) 13.24sec ●
1976   G. Drut (Fr) 13.30sec
1980   T. Munkelt (GDR) 13.39sec
1984 ....

400 Metres Hurdles
1964   R. Cawley (USA) 49.6sec
1968   D. Hemery (GB) 48.1sec
1972   J. Akii-Bua (Uga) 47.82sec
1976   E. Moses (USA) 47.64sec ●
1980   V. Beck (GDR) 48.70sec
1984 ....

3000 Metres Steeplechase
1964   G. Roelants (Bel) 8min 30.8sec
1968   A. Biwott (Ken) 8min 51.0sec
1972   K. Keino (Ken) 8min 23.6sec
1976   A. Garderud (Swe) 8min 08.02sec ●
1980   B. Malinowski (Pol) 8min 09.7sec
1984 ....

4 x 100 Metres Relay
1964   USA 39.0sec
1968   USA 38.2sec
1972   USA 38.19sec ●
1976   USA 38.33sec
1980   USSR 38.26sec
1984 ....

4 x 400 Metres Relay
1964   USA 3min 00.7sec
1968   USA 2min 56.16sec *
1972   Ken 2min 59.83sec
1976   USA 2min 58.65sec
1980   USSR 3min 01.08sec
1984 ....

20 Kilometres Walk
1964   K. Matthews (GB) 1hr 29min 34.0sec
1968   V. Golubnichiy (USSR) 1hr 33min 58.4sec
1972   P. Frenkel (GDR) 1hr 26min 42.4sec
1976   D. Bautista (Mex) 1hr 24min 40.6sec
1980   M. Damilano (Ita) 1hr 23min 35.5sec ●
1984 ....

50 Kilometres Walk
1964   A. Pamich (Ita) 4hr 11min 12.4sec
1968   C. Höhne (GDR) 4hr 20min 13.6sec
1972   B. Kannenburg (Ger) 3hr 56min 11.6sec
1980   H. Gauder (GDR) 3hr 49min 24.0sec ●
1984 ....

High Jump
1964   V. Brumel (USSR) 7ft 1¾ in
1968   D. Fosbury (USA) 7ft 4¼ in
1972   Y. Tarmak (USSR) 7ft 3¾ in
1976   J. Wszola (Pol) 7ft 4½ in/2.25metres
1980   G. Wessig (GDR) 7ft 7½ in/2.36metres ●
1984 ....

Long Jump
1964   L. Davies (GB) 26ft 5¾ in
1968   B. Beamon (USA) 29ft 2½ in 8.90metres *
1972   R. Williams (USA) 27ft 0½ in
1976   A. Robinson (USA) 27ft 4¾ in/8.35metres
1980   L. Danbrowski (GDR) 28ft 0in/8.54metres
1984 ....

Triple Jump
1964   J. Schmidt (Pol) 55ft 3½ in
1968   V. Saneyev (USSR) 57ft 0¾ in/17.39metres ●
1972   V. Saneyev (USSR) 56ft 11¼ in
1976   V. Saneyev (USSR) 56ft 8¾ in/17.29metres
1980   J. Undmae (USSR) 56ft 11¼ in/17.35metres
1984 ....

Pole Vault
1964   F. Hansen (USA) 16ft 8¾ in
1968   B. Seagren (USA) 17ft 8½ in
1972   W. Nordwig (GDR) 18ft 0½ in
1976   T. Slusarski (Pol) 18ft 0½ in/5.50 metres
1980   W. Kozakiewicz (Pol) 18ft 11½ in/5.78metres ●
1984 ....

Shot
1964   D. Long (USA) 66ft 8½ in
1968   R. Matson (USA) 67ft 4¾ in
1972   W. Komar (Pol) 69ft 6in/21.18metres
1976   U. Beyer (GDR) 69ft 0¾ in/21.05metres
1980   V. Kiselyou (USSR) 70ft 0in/21.35metres ●
1984 ....

Discus
1964   A. Oerter (USA) 200ft 1½ in
1968   A. Oerter (USA) 212ft 6½ in/64.78metres
1972   L. Danek (Czh) 211ft 3in
1976   M. Wilkins (USA) 221ft 5½ in/67.50metres ●
1980   V. Rasshchupkin (USSR) 218ft/66.64metres
1984 ....

Javelin
1964   P. Nevala (Fin) 271ft 2in
1968   J. Lusis (USSR) 295ft 7in
1972   K. Wolfermann (Ger) 296ft 10in/90.48metres
1976   M. Nemeth (Hun) 310ft 3¾ in/94.58metres ●
1980   D. Kula (USSR) 299ft 2in/91.20metres
1984 ....

Hammer
1964   R. Klim (USSR) 228ft 10in
1968   G. Zsivotsky (Hun) 240ft 8in
1972   A. Bondarchuk (USSR) 247ft 8in/75.50metres
1976   Y. Sedykh (USSR) 245ft 4in/77.52metres
1980   Y. Sedykh (USSR) 268ft 4in/81.80metres ●
1984 ....

Decathlon
1964   W. Holdorf (Ger) 7887pts
1968   B. Toomey (USA) 8193pts
1972   N. Avilov (USSR) 8454pts
1976   B. Jenner (USA) 8618pts ●
1980   D. Thompson (GB) 8495pts
1984 ....

ATHLETICS – WOMEN

100 Metres
1964   W. Tyus (USA) 11.4sec
1968   W. Tyus (USA) 11.0sec
1972   R. Stecher (GDR) 11.07sec
1976   A. Richter (Ger) 11.08sec
1980   L. Kondratyeva (USSR) 11.06sec
1984 ....

200 Metres
1964   E. McGuire (USA) 23.0sec
1968   I. Szewinska (Pol) 22.5sec
1972   R. Stecher (GDR) 22.40sec
1976   B. Eckert (GDR) 22.37sec
1980   B. Wockel (GDR) 22.03sec ●
1984   . . . .

400 Metres
1964   B. Cuthbert (Aus) 52.0sec
1968   C. Besson (Fr) 52.0sec
1972   M. Zehrt (GDR) 51.08sec
1976   I. Szewinska (Pol) 49.29sec
1980   M. Koch (GDR) 48.88sec ●
1984   . . . .

800 Metres
1964   A. Packer (GB) 2min 01.1sec
1968   M. Manning (USA) 2min 00.9sec
1972   H. Falck (Ger) 1min 58.6sec
1976   T. Kazankina (USSR) 1min 54.94sec
1980   N. Olizarenko (USSR) 1min 53.5sec ●
1984   . . . .

1500 Metres
1972   L. Bragina (USSR) 4min 01.4sec
1976   T. Kazankina (USSR) 4min 05.48sec
1980   T. Kazankina (USSR) 3min 56.6sec ●
1984   . . . .

100 Metres Hurdles
1972   A. Ehrhardt (GDR) 12.59sec
1976   J. Schaller (GDR) 12.77sec
1980   V. Komisova (USSR) 12.56sec ●
1984   . . . .

4 x 100 Metres Relay
1964   Pol 43.6sec
1968   USA 42.8sec
1972   Ger 42.81sec
1976   GDR 42.55sec
1980   GDR 41.60sec ●
1984   . . . .

4 x 400 Metres Relay
1972   GDR 3min 23.0sec
1976   GDR 3min 19.23sec ●
1980   USSR 3min 20.2sec
1984   . . . .

Pentathlon
1964   I. Press (USSR) 5246pts
1968   I. Becker (Ger) 5098pts
1972   M. Peters (GB) 4801pts
1976   S. Siegl (GDR) 4745pts
1980   N. Tkachenko (USSR) 5083pts
1984   . . . .

High Jump
1964   I. Bolas (Rom) 6ft 2¾in
1968   M. Rezkova (Czh) 5ft 11¾in
1972   U. Meyfarth (Ger) 6ft 3½in/1.92metres
1976   R. Ackermann (GDR) 6ft 4in/1.93metres
1980   S. Simeoni (Ita) 6ft 5½in/1.97metres ●
1984   . . . .

Long Jump
1964   M. Rand (GB) 22ft 2¼in
1968   V. Viscopoleanu (Rom) 22ft 4½in/6.82metres
1972   H. Rosendahl (Ger) 22ft 3in
1976   A. Voight (GDR) 22ft 0¾in/6.72metres
1980   T. Kolpakova (USSR) 23ft 1in/7.06metres ●
1984   . . . .

Shot
1964   T. Press (USSR) 59ft 6in
1968   M. Gummel (GDR) 64ft 4in
1972   N. Chizhova (USSR) 69ft 0in/21.03metres
1976   I. Christova (Bul) 69ft 5in/21.16metres
1980   I. Slupianek (GDR) 73ft 5in/22.41metres ●
1984   . . . .

Discus
1964   T. Press (USSR) 187ft 10½in
1968   L. Manolin (Rom) 191ft 2½in
1972   F. Melnik (USSR) 218ft 7in/66.62metres
1976   E. Schlak (GDR) 226ft 3in/69.00metres
1980   E. Jahl (GDR) 229ft 5in/69.96metres ●
1984   . . . .

Javelin
1964   M. Penes (Rom) 198ft 7½in
1968   A. Nemeth (Hun) 198ft 0½in
1972   R. Fuchs (GDR) 209ft 7in/63.88metres
1976   R. Fuchs (GDR) 216ft 4⅛in/65.94metres
1980   M. Colon (Cub) 224ft 5in/68.40metres ●
1984   . . . .

BASKETBALL

Men
1964   USA
1968   USA
1972   USSR
1976   USA
1980   Yugoslavia
1984   . . . .

Women
1976   USSR
1980   USSR
1984   . . . .

BOXING

Light Flyweight
1968   F. Rodriguez (Ven)
1972   G. Gedo (Hun)
1976   J. Hernandez (Cub)
1980   S. Sabyrov (USSR)
1984   . . . .

Flyweight
1964   F. Atzori (Ita)
1968   R. Delgado (Mex)
1972   G. Kostadinov (Bul)
1976   L. Randolph (USA)
1980   P. Lessov (Bul)
1984   . . . .

Bantamweight
1964   T. Sakurai (Jpn)
1968   V. Sokolov (USSR)
1972   O. Martinez (Cub)
1976   Y. Gu (PRK)
1980   J. Hernandez (Cub)
1984   . . . .

Featherweight
1964   S. Stepashkin (USSR)
1968   A. Roldan (Mex)
1972   B. Kousnetsov (USSR)
1976   A. Herrera (Cub)
1980   R. Fink (GDR)
1984   . . . .

Lightweight
1964   J. Grudzien (Pol)
1968   R. Harris (USA)
1972   J. Szczepanski (Pol)
1976   H. Davis (USA)
1980   A. Herrera (Cub)
1984   . . . .

Light Welterweight
1964   J. Kulej (Pol)
1968   J. Kulej (Pol)
1972   R. Seales (USA)
1976   R. Leonard (USA)
1980   P. Oliva (Ita)
1984   . . . .

Welterweight
1964   M. Kasprzyk (Pol)
1968   M. Wolke (GDR)
1972   E. Correa (Cub)
1976   J. Bachfeld (GDR)
1980   A. Aldama (Cub)
1984   . . . .

Light Middleweight
1964   B. Lagutin (USSR)
1968   B. Lagutin (USSR)
1972   D. Kottysch (Ger)
1976   J. Rybicki (Pol)
1980   A. Martinez (Cub)
1984   . . . .

Middleweight
1964   V. Popenchenko (USSR)
1968   C. Finnegan (GB)
1972   V. Lemechev (USSR)
1976   M. Spinks (USA)
1980   J. Gomez (Cub)
1984   . . . .

Light Heavyweight
1964   C. Pinto (Ita)
1968   D. Poznyak (USSR)
1972   M. Parlov (Yug)
1976   L. Spinks (USA)
1980   S. Kacar (Yug)
1984   . . . .

Heavyweight
1964   J. Frazier (USA)
1968   G. Foreman (USA)
1972   T. Stevenson (Cub)
1976   T. Stevenson (Cub)
1980   T. Stevenson (Cub)
1984   . . . .

* Current World/Olympic record   ● Current Olympic record

CANOEING – MEN

Kayak (Singles) 500 Metres
1976	V. Diba (Rom)	1min 46.41sec
1980	V. Parfenovich (USSR)	1min 43.43sec
1984	....	

Kayak (Pairs) 500 Metres
1976	GDR	1min 35.87sec
1980	USSR	1min 32.38sec
1984	....	

Canadian (Singles) 500 Metres
1976	A. Rogov (USSR)	1min 59.23sec
1980	S. Postrekhin (USSR)	1min 53.37sec
1984	....	

Canadian (Pairs) 500 Metres
1976	USSR	1min 45.81sec
1980	Hun	1min 43.39sec
1984	....	

Kayak (Singles) 1000 Metres
1964	R. Peterson (Swe)	3min 57.13sec
1968	M. Hesz (Hun)	4min 02.63sec
1972	A. Shaparenko (USSR)	3min 48.06sec
1976	R. Helm (GDR)	3min 48.20sec
1980	R. Helm (GDR)	3min 48.77sec
1984	....	

Kayak (Pairs) 1000 Metres
1964	Swe	3min 38.54sec
1968	USSR	3min 37.54sec
1972	USSR	3min 31.23sec
1976	USSR	3min 29.01sec
1980	USSR	3min 26.72sec
1984	....	

Kayak (Fours) 1000 Metres
1964	USSR	3min 14.67sec
1968	Nor	3min 14.38sec
1972	USSR	3min 14.02sec
1976	USSR	3min 08.69sec
1980	GDR	3min 13.76sec
1984	....	

Canadian (Singles) 1000 Metres
1964	J. Eschert (Ger)	4min 35.14sec
1968	T. Tatai (Hun)	4min 36.14sec
1972	I. Patzaichin (Rom)	4min 08.94sec
1976	M. Ljubek (Yug)	4min 09.51sec
1980	L. Lubenov (Bul)	4min 12.38sec
1984	....	

Canadian (Pairs) 1000 Metres
1964	USSR	4min 04.65sec
1968	Rom	4min 07.18sec
1972	USSR	3min 52.60sec
1976	USSR	3min 52.76sec
1980	Rom	3min 47.65sec
1984	....	

CANOEING – WOMEN

Kayak (Singles) 500 Metres
1964	L. Khvedosink (USSR)	2min 12.87sec
1968	L. Pinaeva (USSR)	2min 11.09sec
1972	Y. Ryabchinskaya (USSR)	2min 03.17sec
1976	C. Zirzow (GDR)	2min 01.05sec
1980	B. Fischer (GDR)	1min 57.96sec
1984	....	

Kayak (Pairs) 500 Metres
1964	Ger	1min 56.95sec
1968	Ger	1min 56.44sec
1972	USSR	1min 53.50sec
1976	USSR	1min 51.15sec
1980	GDR	1min 43.88sec
1984	....	

CYCLING

1,000 Metres Sprint
1964	G. Pettenella (Ita)	13.69sec
1968	D. Morelon (Fr)	10.68sec
1972	D. Morelon (Fr)	11.69sec
1976	A. Tkak (Czh)	10.78sec
1980	L. Hesslich (GDR)	11.40sec
1984	....	

(Times for last 200 metres)

1,000 Metres Time Trial
1964	P. Sercu (Bel)	1min 09.59sec
1968	P. Trentin (Fr)	1min 03.91sec
1972	N. Fredborg (Den)	1min 06.44sec
1976	K. Grunke (GDR)	1min 05.927sec
1980	L. Thoms (GDR)	1min 02.955sec *
1984	....	

4,000 Metres Team Pursuit
1964	Ger	4min 35.67sec
1968	Den	4min 22.44sec
1972	Ger	4min 22.14sec
1976	Ger	4min 21.06sec
1980	USSR	4min 15.70sec
1984	....	

4,000 Metres Individual Pursuit
1964	J. Daler (Czh)	5min 04.75sec
1968	D. Rebillard (Fr)	4min 41.71sec
1972	K. Knudsen (Nor)	4min 45.74sec
1976	G. Braun (Ger)	4min 47.61sec
1980	R. Dill-Bundi (Swi)	4min 35.66sec
1984	....	

Road Race (Individual)
1964	M. Zanin (Ita)	4hr 39min 51.63sec
1968	P. Vianelli (Ita)	4hr 41min 25.24sec
1972	H. Kuyper (Neth)	4hr 14min 37.0sec
1976	B. Johansson (Swe)	4hr 46min 52.0sec
1980	S. Sukhoruchenkov (USSR)	4hr 48min 28.9sec
1984	....	

Road Race (Team)
1964	Neth	2hr 26min 13.1sec (109.89km)
1968	Neth	2hr 07min 49.0sec (102km)
1972	USSR	2hr 11min 17.8sec (100km)
1976	USSR	2hr 08min 53.0sec (100km)
1980	USSR	2hr 01min 21.7sec (101km)
1984	....	

EQUESTRIAN EVENTS

Grand Prix/Individual Show Jumping
1964	P. d'Oriola (Fr)
1968	W. Steinkraus (USA)
1972	G. Mancinelli (Ita)
1976	A. Schockemoehle (Ger)
1980	J. Kowalcyzyk (Pol)
1984	....

Grand Prix/Team Show Jumping
1964	Germany
1968	Canada
1972	Germany
1976	France
1980	USSR
1984	....

Grand Prix/Individual Dressage
1964	H. Chammartin (Swi)
1968	I. Kizimov (USSR)
1972	L. Linsenhoff (Ger)
1976	C. Stueckelberger (Swi)
1980	E. Theurer (Aut)
1984	....

Grand Prix/Team Dressage
1964	Germany
1968	Germany
1972	USSR
1976	Germany
1980	USSR
1984	....

3-Day Individual Event
1964	M. Checcoli (Ita)
1968	J. Guyon (Fr)
1972	R. Meade (GB)
1976	E. Coffin (USA)
1980	F. Roman (Ita)
1984	....

3-Day Team Event
1964	Italy
1968	GB
1972	GB
1976	USA
1980	USSR
1984	....

FENCING – MEN

Foil/Individual
1964	E. Franke (Pol)
1968	I. Drimba (Rom)
1972	W. Woyda (Pol)
1976	F. Dal Zotto (Ita)
1980	V. Smirnov (USSR)
1984	....

Foil/Team
1964	USSR
1968	France
1972	Poland
1976	Germany
1980	France
1984	....

Epée/Individual
1964	G. Kriss (USSR)
1968	G. Kulcsar (Hun)
1972	C. Fenyvesi (Hun)
1976	A. Pusch (Ger)
1980	J. Harmenberg (Swe)
1984	. . . .

Epée/Team
1964	Hungary
1968	Hungary
1972	Hungary
1976	Sweden
1980	France
1984	. . . .

Sabre/Individual
1964	T. Pezsa (Hun)
1968	J. Pawlowski (Pol)
1972	V. Sidiak (USSR)
1976	V. Korvopouskov (USSR)
1980	V. Korvopouskov (USSR)
1984	. . . .

Sabre/Team
1964	USSR
1968	USSR
1972	Italy
1976	USSR
1980	USSR
1984	. . . .

FENCING – WOMEN

Foil/Individual
1964	I. Rejto (Hun)
1968	E. Novikova (USSR)
1972	A. Lonzi (Ita)
1976	I. Schwarczenberger (Hun)
1980	P. Trinquet (Fr)
1984	. . . .

Foil/Team
1964	Hungary
1968	USSR
1972	USSR
1976	USSR
1980	France
1984	. . . .

GYMNASTICS – MEN

Combined Exercises
1964	Y. Endo (Jpn)
1968	S. Kato (Jpn)
1972	S. Kato (Jpn)
1976	N. Andrianov (USSR)
1980	A. Dityatin (USSR)
1984	. . . .

Floor Exercises
1964	F. Menichelli (Ita)
1968	S. Kato (Jpn)
1972	N. Andrianov (USSR)
1976	N. Andrianov (USSR)
1980	R. Bruckner (GDR)
1984	. . . .

Pommel/Horse
1964	M. Cerar (Yug)
1968	M. Cerar (Yug)
1972	V. Klimenko (USSR)
1976	Z. Magyar (Hun)
1980	Z. Magyar (Hun)
1984	. . . .

Rings
1964	T. Hayata (Jpn)
1968	A. Nakayama (Jpn)
1972	A. Nakayama (Jpn)
1976	N. Andrianov (USSR)
1980	A. Dityatin (USSR)
1984	. . . .

Long Horse/Vault
1964	H. Yamashita (Jpn)
1968	M. Voronin (USSR)
1972	K. Koeste (GDR)
1976	N. Andrianov (USSR)
1980	N. Andrianov (USSR)
1984	. . . .

Parallel Bars
1964	Y. Endo (Jpn)
1968	A. Nakayama (Jpn)
1972	S. Kato (Jpn)
1976	S. Kato (Jpn)
1980	A. Tkachyov (USSR)
1984	. . . .

Horizontal Bars
1964	B. Shakhlin (USSR)
1968	M. Voronin (USSR) / A. Nakayama (Jpn)
1972	M. Tsukahara (Jpn)
1976	M. Tsukahara (Jpn)
1980	S. Deltchev (Bul)
1984	. . . .

Team
1964	Japan
1968	Japan
1972	Japan
1976	Japan
1980	USSR
1984	. . . .

GYMNASTICS – WOMEN

Combined Exercises
1964	V. Caslavska (Czh)
1968	V. Caslavska (Czh)
1972	L. Tourischeva (USSR)
1976	N. Comaneci (Rom)
1980	E. Davydova (USSR)
1984	. . . .

Floor Exercises
1964	L. Latynina (USSR)
1968	L. Petrik (USSR) / V. Caslavska (Czh)
1972	O. Korbut (USSR)
1976	N. Kim (USSR)
1980	N. Kim (USSR) / N. Comaneci (Rom)
1984	. . . .

Asymmetrical Bars
1964	P. Astakhova (USSR)
1968	V. Caslavska (Czh)
1972	K. Janz (GDR)
1976	N. Comaneci (Rom)
1980	M. Gnauck (GDR)
1984	. . . .

Beam
1964	V. Caslavska (Czh)
1968	N. Kuchinskaya (USSR)
1972	O. Korbut (USSR)
1976	N. Comaneci (Rom)
1980	N. Comaneci (Rom)
1984	. . . .

Horse/Vault
1964	V. Caslavska (Czh)
1968	V. Caslavska (Czh)
1972	K. Janz (GDR)
1976	N. Kim (USSR)
1980	N. Shaposhnikova (USSR)
1984	. . . .

Team
1964	USSR
1968	USSR
1972	USSR
1976	USSR
1980	USSR
1984	. . . .

HANDBALL

Men
1972	Yugoslavia
1976	USSR
1980	GDR
1984	. . . .

Women
1976	USSR
1980	USSR
1984	. . . .

HOCKEY

Men
1964	India
1968	Pakistan
1972	Germany
1976	New Zealand
1980	India
1984	. . . .

Women
1964	–
1968	–
1972	–
1976	–
1980	Zimbabwe
1984	. . . .

JUDO

Lightweight
1964	T. Nakatani (Jpn)
1972	T. Kawaguchi (Jpn)
1976	H. Rodriguez (Cub)

Bantamweight (60kg)
1980   T. Rey (Fr)
1984   ....

Welterweight
1972   K. Nomura (Jpn)
1976   V. Nevzorov (USSR)

Featherweight (65kg)
1980   N. Salodukhin (USSR)
1984   ....

Middleweight
1964   I. Okano (Jpn)
1972   S. Sekine (Jpn)
1976   I. Sonoda (Jpn)

Lightweight (71kg)
1980   E. Gamba (Ita)
1984   ....

Light Heavyweight
1972   S. Chachoshvili (USSR)
1976   K. Ninomiya (Jpn)

Light Middleweight (78kg)
1980   S. Khabareli (USSR)
1984   ....

Heavyweight
1964   I. Inokuma (Jpn)
1972   W. Ruska (Neth)
1976   S. Novikov (USSR)

Middleweight (86kg)
1980   J. Roethlisberger (Swi)
1984   ....

Open
1964   A. Geesink (Neth)
1972   W. Ruska (Neth)
1976   H. Uemura (Jpn)
1980   D. Lorenz (GDR)
1984   ....

Light Heavyweight (95kg)
1980   R. Van de Walle (Bel)
1984   ....

Heavyweight (over 95kg)
1980   A. Parisi (Fr)
1984   ....

MODERN PENTATHLON

Modern Pentathlon Individual
1964   F. Toerek (Hun)
1968   B. Ferm (Swe)
1972   A. Balczo (Hun)
1976   J. Pyciak-Peciak (Pol)
1980   A. Starostin (USSR)
1984   ....

Modern Pentathlon Team
1964   USSR
1968   Hungary
1972   USSR
1976   GB
1980   USSR
1984   ....

ROWING – MEN
2,000 METRES

Single Sculls
1964   V. Ivanov (USSR) 8min 22.51sec
1968   H. Wienese (Neth) 7min 47.80sec
1972   Y. Malishev (USSR) 7min 10.12sec
1976   P. Karppinen (Fin) 7min 29.03sec
1980   P. Karppinen (Fin) 7min 09.61sec
1984   ....

Double Sculls
1964   USSR 7min 10.66sec
1968   USSR 6min 51.82sec
1972   USSR 7min 01.77sec
1976   Norway 7min 13.20sec
1080   GDR 6min 24.33sec
1984   ....

Coxless Pair
1964   Canada 7min 32.94sec
1968   GDR 7min 26.56sec
1972   GDR 6min 53.16sec
1976   GDR 7min 23.31sec
1980   GDR 6min 48.01sec
1984   ....

Coxed Pair
1964   USA 8min 21.23sec
1968   Italy 8min 04.81sec
1972   GDR 7min 17.25sec
1976   GDR 7min 58.99sec
1980   GDR 7min 02.54sec
1984   ....

Quadruple Sculls
1976   GDR 6min 18.35sec
1980   GDR 5min 49.81sec
1984   ....

Coxless Fours
1964   Denmark 6min 59.30sec
1968   GDR 6min 39.18sec
1972   GDR 6min 24.27sec
1976   GDR 6min 37.42sec
1980   GDR 6min 08.17sec
1984   ....

Coxed Fours
1964   Germany 7min 00.44sec
1968   New Zealand 6min 45.62sec
1972   Germany 6min 31.85sec
1976   USSR 6min 40.22sec
1980   GDR 6min 14.51sec
1984   ....

Eights
1964   USA 6min 18.23sec
1968   Germany 6min 07.00sec
1972   New Zealand 6min 08.94sec
1976   GDR 5min 58.29sec
1980   GDR 5min 49.05sec
1984   ....

ROWING – WOMEN
(1,000 METRES)

Single Sculls
1976   C. Scheiblich (GDR) 4min 05.56sec
1980   S. Toma (Rom) 3min 40.69sec
1984   ....

Double Sculls
1976   Bulgaria 3min 44.36sec
1980   USSR 3min 16.27sec
1984   ....

Coxless Pair
1976   Bulgaria 4min 01.22sec
1980   GDR 3min 30.49sec
1984   ....

Coxed Pair
1976   GDR 3min 45.08sec
1984   ....

Quadruple Sculls
1976   GDR 3min 29.99sec
1980   GDR 3min 15.32sec
1984   ....

Coxed Fours
1976   GDR 3min 45.08sec
1980   GDR 3min 19.27sec
1984   ....

Eights
1976   GDR 3min 33.32sec
1980   GDR 3min 03.32sec
1984   ....

SHOOTING

Olympic Trap/Clay Pigeon
1964   E. Mattarelli (Ita)
1968   R. Braithwaite (GB)
1972   A. Scalzone (Ita)
1976   D. Haldeman (USA)
1980   L. Giovannetti (Ita)
1984   ....

Running Game
1972   L. Zhelezniak (USSR)
1976   A. Gazov (USSR)
1980   I. Sokolov (USSR)
1984   ....

Rapid Fire Pistol
1964   P. Linnosvuo (Fin)
1968   J. Zapedzki (Pol)
1972   J. Zapedzki (Pol)
1976   N. Klaar (GDR)
1980   C. Ion (Rom)
1984   ....

Skeet
1968   E. Petrov (USSR)
1972   K. Wirnhier (Ger)
1976   J. Panacek (Czh)
1980   H. Rasmussen (Den)
1984   ....

Free Pistol
1964   V. Markkanen (Fin)
1968   G. Kosykh (USSR)
1972   R. Skanakar (Swe)
1976   U. Potteck (GDR)
1980   A. Melentev (USSR)
1984   ....

Small Bore Rifle – Prone Position
1964   L. Hammerl (Hun)
1968   J. Kurka (Czh)
1972   Ho Jun Li (PRK)
1976   K. Smieszek (Ger)
1980   K. Varga (Hun)
1984   . . . .

Small Bore Rifle – 3 Positions
1964   L. Wigger (USA)
1968   B. Klingner (Ger)
1972   J. Writer (USA)
1976   L. Bassham (USA)
1980   V. Vlasov (USSR)
1984   . . . .

Air-rifle – Men
1984   . . . .

Air-rifle – Women
1984   . . . .

Pistol – Women
1984   . . . .

Small Bore Rifle – Women
1984   . . . .

SWIMMING – MEN

100 Metres Freestyle
1964   D. Schollander (USA) 53.4sec
1968   M. Wenden (Aus) 52.2sec
1972   M. Spitz (USA) 51.22sec
1976   J. Montgomery (USA) 49.99sec ●
1980   J. Waithe (GDR) 50.40sec
1984   . . . .

200 Metres Freestyle
1968   M. Wenden (Aus) 1min 55.2sec
1972   M. Spitz (USA) 1min 52.78sec
1976   B. Furniss (USA) 1min 50.29sec
1980   S. Kopliakov (USSR) 1min 49.81sec ●
1984   . . . .

400 Metres Freestyle
1964   D. Schollander (USA) 4min 12.2sec
1968   M. Burton (USA) 4min 09.0sec
1972   B. Cooper (Aus) 4min 00.27sec†
1976   B. Goodell (USA) 3min 51.93sec
1980   V. Salnikov (USSR) 3min 51.31sec ●
1984   . . . .
† R. Demont (USA) finished first in 4min
00.26sec, but was disqualified

1,500 Metres Freestyle
1964   B. Windle (Aus) 17min 01.7sec
1968   M. Burton (USA) 16min 38.9sec
1972   M. Burton (USA) 15min 52.58sec
1976   B. Goodell (USA) 15min 02.40sec
1980   V. Salnikov (USSR) 14min 58.27sec ●
1984   . . . .

100 Metres Backstroke
1968   R. Matthes (GDR) 58.7sec
1972   R. Matthes (GDR) 56.58sec
1976   J. Naber (USA) 55.49sec ●
1980   B. Baron (Swe) 56.53sec
1984   . . . .

200 Metres Backstroke
1964   J. Graef (USA) 2min 10.3sec
1968   R. Matthes (GDR) 2min 09.6sec
1972   R. Matthes (GDR) 2min 02.82sec
1976   J. Naber (USA) 1min 59.19sec ●
1980   S. Wladar (Hun) 2min 01.93sec
1984   . . . .

100 Metres Breaststroke
1968   D. McKenzie (USA) 1min 07.7sec
1972   N. Taguchi (Jpn) 1min 04.94sec
1976   J. Hencken (USA) 1min 03.11sec ●
1980   D. Goodhew (GB) 1min 03.34sec
1984   . . . .

200 Metres Breaststroke
1964   I. O'Brien (Aus) 2min 27.8sec
1968   F. Munoz (Mex) 2min 28.7sec
1972   J. Hencken (USA) 2min 21.55sec
1976   D. Wilkie (GB) 2min 15.11sec ●
1980   R. Zulpa (USSR) 2min 15.85sec
1984   . . . .

100 Metres Butterfly
1968   D. Russell (USA) 55.97sec
1972   M. Spitz (USA) 54.27sec ●
1976   M. Vogel (USA) 54.35sec
1980   P. Arvidsson (Swe) 54.92sec
1984   . . . .

200 Metres Butterfly
1964   K. Berry (Aus) 2min 06.6sec
1968   C. Robie (USA) 2min 08.7sec
1972   M. Spitz (USA) 2min 00.70sec
1976   M. Bruner (USA) 1min 59.23sec ●
1980   S. Fesenko (USSR) 1min 59.76sec
1984   . . . .

200 Metres Individual Medley
1968   C. Hickcox (USA) 2min 12.0sec
1972   G. Larsson (Swe) 2min 07.17sec ●
1984   . . . .

400 Metres Individual Medley
1964   D. Roth (USA) 4min 45.4sec
1968   C. Hickcox (USA) 4min 48.4sec
1972   G. Larsson (Swe) 4min 31.98sec
1976   R. Strachan (USA) 4min 23.68sec
1980   A. Sidorenko (USSR) 4min 22.89sec ●
1984   . . . .

4 x 100 Metres Freestyle Relay
1964   USA 3min 33.2sec
1968   USA 3min 31.7sec
1972   USA 3min 26.42sec ●
1984   . . . .

4 x 200 Metres Freestyle Relay
1964   USA 7min 52.1sec
1968   USA 7min 52.3sec
1972   USA 7min 35.78sec
1976   USA 7min 23.22sec ●
1980   USSR 7min 23.50sec
1984   . . . .

4 x 100 Metres Medley Relay
1964   USA 3min 58.4sec
1968   USA 3min 54.9sec
1972   USA 3min 48.16sec
1976   USA 3min 42.22sec ●
1980   Australia 3min 45.70sec
1984   . . . .

Springboard Diving
1964   K. Sitzberger (USA)
1968   B. Wrightson (USA)
1972   V. Vasin (USSR)
1976   P. Boggs (USA)
1980   A. Portnov (USSR)
1984   . . . .

Highboard Diving
1964   R. Webster (USA)
1968   K. Dibiasi (Ita)
1972   K. Dibiasi (Ita)
1976   K. Dibiasi (Ita)
1980   F. Hoffmann (GDR)
1984   . . . .

Water Polo
1964   Hungary
1968   Yugoslavia
1972   USSR
1976   Hungary
1980   USSR
1984   . . . .

SWIMMING – WOMEN

100 Metres Freestyle
1964   D. Fraser (Aus) 59.5sec
1968   J. Henne (USA) 1min 00.0sec
1972   S. Neilson (USA) 58.59sec
1976   K. Ender (GDR) 55.65sec
1980   B. Krause (GDR) 54.79sec *
1984   . . . .

200 Metres Freestyle
1968   D. Meyer (USA) 2min 10.5sec
1972   S. Gould (Aus) 2min 03.56sec
1976   K. Ender (GDR) 1min 59.26sec
1980   B. Krause (GDR) 1min 58.33sec*
1984   . . . .

400 Metres Freestyle
1964   V. Duenkel (USA) 4min 43.3sec
1968   D. Meyer (USA) 4min 31.8sec
1972   S. Gould (Aus) 4min 19.04sec
1976   P. Thumer (GDR) 4min 09.89sec
1980   I. Diers (GDR) 4min 08.76sec ●
1984   . . . .

800 Metres Freestyle
1968   D. Meyer (USA) 9min 24.0sec
1972   K. Rothammer (USA) 8min 53.68sec
1976   P. Thumer (GDR) 8min 37.14sec
1980   M. Ford (Aus) 8min 28.90sec ●
1984   . . . .

100 Metres Backstroke
1964   C. Ferguson (USA) 1min 07.7sec
1968   K. Hall (USA) 1min 06.2sec
1972   M. Belote (USA) 1min 05.78sec
1976   U. Richter (GDR) 1min 01.83sec
1980   R. Reinisch (GDR) 1min 00.86sec
1984   . . . .

200 Metres Backstroke
1968   P. Watson (USA) 2min 24.8sec
1972   M. Belote (USA) 2min 19.9sec
1976   U. Richter (GDR) 2min 13.43sec
1980   R. Reinisch (GDR) 2min 11.77sec ●
1984   . . . .

* Current World/Olympic record   ● Current Olympic record

00 Metres Breaststroke
968 D. Bjedov (Yug) 1min 15.8sec
972 C. Carr (USA) 1min 13.58sec
976 H. Anka (GDR) 1min 11.16sec
980 U. Geweniger (GDR) 1min 10.22sec
984 ....

200 Metres Breaststroke
964 G. Prozumenschikova (USSR) 2min 46.4sec
968 S. Wichman (USA) 2min 44.4sec
972 B. Whitfield (Aus) 2min 41.71sec
976 M. Koshevaia (USSR) 2min 33.35sec
980 L. Kachushite (USSR) 2min 29.54sec ●
984 ....

100 Metres Butterfly
964 S. Stouder (USA) 1min 04.7sec
968 L. McClements (Aus) 1min 05.5sec
972 M. Aoki (Jpn) 1min 03.34sec
976 K. Ender (GDR) 1min 00.13sec ●
980 C. Metschuck (GDR) 1min 00.42sec
984 ....

200 Metres Butterfly
1968 A. Kok (Neth) 2min 24.7sec
1972 K. Moe (USA) 2min 15.57sec
1976 A. Pollack (GDR) 2min 11.41sec
1980 I. Geissler (GDR) 2min 10.44sec ●
1984 ....

200 Metres Individual Medley
1968 C. Kolb (Aus) 2min 24.97sec
1972 S. Gould (Aus) 2min 23.07sec ●
1984 ....

400 Metres Individual Medley
1964 D. de Varona (USA) 5min 18.7sec
1968 C. Kolb (USA) 5min 08.5sec
1972 G. Neall (Aus) 5min 02.97sec
1976 U. Tauber (GDR) 4min 42.77sec
1980 P. Schneider (GDR) 4min 36.29sec ●
1984 ....

4 x 100 Metres Freestyle Relay
1964 USA 4min 03.8sec
1968 USA 4min 02.5sec
1972 USA 3min 55.19sec
1976 USA 3min 44.82sec
1980 GDR 3min 42.71sec*
1984 ....

4 x 100 Metres Medley Relay
1964 USA 4min 33.9sec
1968 USA 4min 28.3sec
1972 USA 4min 20.75sec
1976 GDR 4min 07.95sec
1980 GDR 4min 06.67sec ●
1984 ....

Synchronised Swimming
1984 ....

Springboard
1964 I. Engel-Kramer (Ger)
1968 S. Gossick (USA)
1972 M. King (USA)
1976 J. Chandler (USA)
1980 I. Kalinina (USSR)
1984 ....

Highboard
1964 L. Bush (USA)
1968 M. Duchkova (Czh)
1972 U. Knape (Swe)
1976 E. Vaytsekhovskaya (USSR)
1980 M. Jaschke (GDR)
1984 ....

VOLLEYBALL

Men
1964 USSR
1968 USSR
1972 Japan
1976 Poland
1980 USSR
1984 ....

Women
1964 Japan
1968 USSR
1972 USSR
1976 Japan
1980 USSR
1984 ....

WEIGHTLIFTING

Flyweight
1972 Z. Smalcerz (Pol) 743¾lb
1976 A. Voronin (USSR) 242.5kg/534½lb
1980 K. Osmanaliev (USSR) 245kg/540lb ●
1984 ....

Bantamweight
1964 A. Vakhonin (USSR) 787¾lb
1968 M. Nassiri (Irn) 809¾lb
1972 I. Foeldi (Hun) 831¾lb
1976 N. Nurikyan (Bul) 262.5kg/578½lb
1980 D. Nunez (Cub) 275kg/606¼lb ●
1984 ....

Featherweight
1964 Y. Miyake (Jpn) 876lb
1968 Y. Miyake (Jpn) 865lb
1972 N. Nurikyan (Bul) 887lb
1976 N. Kolesnikov (USSR) 285kg/628¼lb
1980 V. Mazin (USSR) 290kg/639¼lb ●
1984 ....

Lightweight
1964 W. Baszanowski (Pol) 953¼lb
1968 W. Baszanowski (Pol) 964¼lb
1972 M. Kirzhinov (USSR) 1014 lb
1976 P. Korol (USSR) 305kg/627¼lb†
1980 Y. Roussev (Bul) 342.5kg/755lb*
1984 ....

†Z. Kaczmarck finished in first place with 307.5kg/677¾lb but was subsequently disqualified

Middleweight
1964 H. Zdrazila (Czh) 980¾lb
1968 V. Kurentsov (USSR) 1,046¾lb
1972 Y. Bikov (Bul) 1,068¾lb
1976 Y. Mitkov (Bul) 335kg/738¼lb
1980 A. Zlatev (Bul) 360kg/793½lb ●
1984 ....

Light Heavyweight
1964 R. Plyukfelder (USSR) 1,047lb
1968 B. Selitsky (USSR) 1,068¾lb
1972 L. Jensen (Nor) 1,118¾lb
1976 V. Shary (USSR) 365kg/804¼lb
1980 Y. Vardanyan (USSR) 400kg/881¾lb ●
1984 ....

Middle Heavyweight
1964 V. Golovanov (USSR) 1,074½lb
1968 K. Kangasniemi (Fin) 1,140½lb
1972 A. Nikolov (Bul) 1,157lb
1976 D. Rigert (USSR) 382.5kg/843¼lb
1980 P. Baczako (Hun) 377.5kg/832¼lb
1984 ....

Heavyweight
1964 L. Zhabotinsky (USSR) 1,262¾lb ●
1968 L. Zhabotinsky (USSR) 1,261¾lb
1972 J. Talts (USSR) 1,278¼lb
1976 Y. Zaitsev (USSR) 385kg/848¾lb†
1980 L. Taranenko (USSR) 422.5kg/931¼lb
1984 ....

†V. Khristov (Bul) finished first with 400kg/881¼lb but was subsequently disqualified

Super Heavyweight
1972 V. Alexeev (USSR) 1,410¾lb
1976 V. Alexeev (USSR) 440kg/969¾lb
1980 S. Rakhamanov (USSR) 440kg/969¾lb
1984 ....

1980 new category
up to 100kg: O. Zaremba (Czh) 395kg/870¾lb

(Weights from 1976 taken from combination of Snatch and Jerk lifts)

WRESTLING – FREESTYLE

Light-flyweight
1972 R. Dmitriev (USSR)
1976 K. Issaev (Bul)
1980 C. Pollio (Ita)
1984 ....

Flyweight
1964 Y. Yoshida (Jpn)
1968 S. Nakato (Jpn)
1972 K. Kato (Jpn)
1976 Y. Takado (Jpn)
1980 A. Beloglazov (USSR)
1984 ....

Bantamweight
1964 Y. Uetake (Jpn)
1968 Y. Uetake (Jpn)
1972 H. Yanagida (Jpn)
1976 V. Umin (USSR)
1980 S. Beloglazov (USSR)
1984 ....

Featherweight
1964 O. Watanabe (Jpn)
1968 M. Kaneko (Jpn)
1972 Z. Abdulbekov (USSR)
1976 J-M. Yang (SKR)
1980 M. Abushev (USSR)
1984 ....

urrent World/Olympic record ● Current Olympic record

Lightweight
1964	E. Valtshev (Bul)
1968	A. Mohaved Ardabili (Irn)
1972	D. Gable (USA)
1976	P. Pinigin (USSR)
1980	M. Absaidov (USSR)
1984	....

Welterweight
1964	I. Ogan (Tur)
1968	M. Atalay (Tur)
1972	W. Wells (USA)
1976	J. Date (Jpn)
1980	V. Raitchev (Bul)
1984	....

Middleweight
1964	P. Gardshev (Bul)
1968	B. Gurevitch (USSR)
1972	L. Tediashvili (USSR)
1976	J. Peterson (USA)
1980	I. Abilov (Bul)
1984	....

Light Heavyweight
1964	A. Medved (USSR)
1968	A. Ayik (Tur)
1972	B. Peterson (USA)
1976	L. Tediashvili (USSR)
1980	S. Oganesyan (USSR)
1984	....

Heavyweight
1964	A. Ivanitsky (USSR)
1968	A. Medved (USSR)
1972	I. Yarygin (USSR)
1976	I. Yarygin (USSR)
1980	I. Mate (Yug)
1984	....

Super Heavyweight
1972	A. Medved (USSR)
1976	S. Andiev (USSR)
1980	S. Andiev (USSR)
1984	....

WRESTLING – GRECO-ROMAN

Light-Flyweight
1972	G. Berceanu (Rom)
1976	A. Shumakov (USSR)
1980	Z. Ushkempirov (USSR)
1984	....

Flyweight
1964	T. Hanahara (Jpn)
1968	P. Kirov (Bul)
1972	P. Kirov (Bul)
1976	V. Konstantinov (USSR)
1980	V. Blagidze (USSR)
1984	....

Bantamweight
1964	M. Ichiguchi (Jpn)
1968	J. Varga (Hun)
1972	R. Kazakov (USSR)
1976	P. Ukkola (Fin)
1980	S. Serikov (USSR)
1984	....

Featherweight
1964	I. Polyak (Hun)
1968	R. Rurua (USSR)
1972	G. Markov (Bul)
1976	K. Lipien (Pol)
1980	S. Migiakis (Gre)
1984	....

Lightweight
1964	K. Ayvaz (Tur)
1968	M. Munemura (Jpn)
1972	S. Khismutdinov (USSR)
1976	S. Nalbandyan (USSR)
1980	S. Rusu (Rom)
1984	....

Welterweight
1964	A. Koleslov (USSR)
1968	R. Vesper (GDR)
1972	V. Macha (Czh)
1976	A. Bykov (USSR)
1980	F. Kocsis (Hun)
1984	....

Middleweight
1964	B. Simic (Yug)
1968	L. Metz (GDR)
1972	C. Hegedus (Hun)
1976	M. Petkovic (Yug)
1980	G. Korban (USSR)
1984	....

Light Heavyweight
1964	R. Radev (Bul)
1968	R. Radev (Bul)
1972	V. Rezantsev (USSR)
1976	V. Rezantsev (USSR)
1980	N. Nottny (Hun)
1984	....

Heavyweight
1964	I. Kozma (Hun)
1968	I. Kozma (Hun)
1972	N. Martinescu (Rom)
1976	N. Bolboshin (USSR)
1980	G. Railkov (Bul)
1984	....

Super Heavyweight
1972	A. Roschin (USSR)
1976	A. Kolchinski (USSR)
1980	A. Kolchinski (USSR)
1984	....

YACHTING

5.5 Metres
1964	Australia
1968	Sweden
1984	....

Tempest
1972	USSR 28.1pts
1976	Sweden 14.00pts
1984	....

Soling
1972	USA 8.7pts
1976	Denmark 46.70pts
1980	Denmark 23.00pts
1984	....

Flying Dutchman
1964	New Zealand 6255pts
1968	GB 3.0pts
1972	GB 22.7pts
1976	Germany 34.70pts
1980	Spain 19.00pts
1984	....

Dragon
1964	Denmark 5854pts
1968	USA 6.0pts
1972	Australia 13.7pts
1984	....

Star
1964	Bahamas 5664pts
1968	USA 14.4pts
1972	Australia 28.1pts
1980	USSR 24.70pts
1984	....

Tornado
1976	GB 18.0pts
1980	Brazil 21.40pts
1984	....

Finn
1964	Germany 7638pts
1968	USSR 11.7pts
1972	France 58.0pts
1976	GDR 35.40pts
1980	Finland 36.70pts
1984	....

470
1976	Germany 42.40pts
1980	Brazil 36.40pts
1984	....

Windsurfing
1984	....

Picture Credits

Allsport Photographic Ltd
6, 7, 8-9, 20, 21, 22, 28, 29, 36, 37, 38, 39, 40, 41, 42-3, 46, 47, 52, 53, 54, 55, 59, 62, 63, 64, 65, 74, 82, 84, 86, 88, 90-1, 96-7, 98, 101, 102, 103, 104, 106, 107, 108-9, 111, 112, 113, 114, 115, 118, 120, 122, 123, 130, 131, 134-5, jacket cover

Leo Mason 24
Presse-Foto Baumann
8, 9, 10, 11, 12, 13, 14, 15, 16, 17, 18-19, 22, 23, 24, 25, 26-7, 30, 31, 32, 33, 34-5, 36, 38, 40, 44, 45, 46, 48, 49, 50-1, 52-3, 56, 57, 58, 60-1, 66, 67, 68, 69, 70, 71, 72, 73, 74, 75, 76, 77, 78, 79, 80, 81, 82-3, 84-5, 86, 87, 88, 89, 92, 93, 94, 95, 98, 99, 100, 104, 105, 110, 110-11, 116, 117, 119, 121, 124, 125, 126-7, 128, 129, 132-3

Ted Thai/Time Magazine 4-5